Building Wireless Community Networks

Building Wireless Community Networks

Rob Flickenger

O'REILLY®

Beijing · Cambridge · Farnham · Köln · Paris · Sebastopol · Taipei · Tokyo

Building Wireless Community Networks
by Rob Flickenger

Copyright © 2002 O'Reilly & Associates, Inc. All rights reserved.
Printed in the United States of America.

Published by O'Reilly & Associates, Inc., 1005 Gravenstein Highway North,
Sebastopol, CA 95472.

O'Reilly & Associates books may be purchased for educational, business, or sales pro-
motional use. Online editions are also available for most titles (*safari.oreilly.com*). For
more information contact our corporate/institutional sales department: (800) 998-9938
or *corporate@oreilly.com*.

Editor:	Sue Miller
Production Editor:	Leanne Clarke Soylemez
Cover Designer:	Ellie Volckhausen
Interior Designer:	David Futato

Printing History:

January 2002:	First Edition.

ISBN: 0-596-00204-1

[C]

Table of Contents

Preface

Building Wireless Community Networks is about getting people connected to one another. Wireless technology is being used right now to connect neighborhoods, businesses, and schools to the vast, massively interconnected, and nebulous entity known as the Internet. One of the goals of this book is to help you get your community "unplugged" and online, using inexpensive off-the-shelf equipment.

A secondary but critical goal of this book is to come to terms with exactly what is meant by *community*. It might refer to your college campus, where many people own their own laptops and want to share files and access to the Internet. Your idea of community could encompass your apartment building or neighborhood, where broadband Internet access may not even be available. This book is intended to get you thinking about what is involved in getting people in your community connected, and it will demonstrate working examples of how to make these connections possible.

Audience

This book describes some solutions to the current (but rapidly changing) problem of building a wireless network for community use. It is *not* intended to be a design guide for wireless companies and ISPs, although I hope they find the information in it useful (and at least a little bit entertaining).

This book is intended for the technical user who is interested in bringing wireless high-speed network access to wherever it's needed. This could include extending Internet connectivity to areas where other access (such as DSL or cable) isn't available. It could also include setting up access at a school, where structures were built long before anyone thought about running cables and lines into classrooms. This book should also be useful for people interested in learning about how dozens of groups around the planet are providing wireless access in their own communities. The story of wireless network access is still in its infancy, but it is already full of fascinating twists and turns (never mind its potential!). I hope to communicate what I've learned of this story to you.

Organization

Early chapters of this book introduce basic wireless concepts and essential network services, while later chapters focus on specific aspects of building your own wireless network. Experienced users may prefer to skip around rather than read this book from cover to cover, so here's an overview of each chapter:

- Chapter 1, *Wireless Community Networks*, gives a brief history of the state of wireless connectivity and some ideas (and warnings) about how things might proceed.

- Chapter 2, *Defining Project Scope*, is an overview of many important logistical considerations you will face in designing your own network; it describes some tools that may make your job easier.

- Chapter 3, *Network Layout*, provides a detailed description of critical network components that you will need to provide to your users. Network layout and security are also addressed.

- Chapter 4, *Using Access Points*, details how to use wireless access point hardware effectively.

- Chapter 5, *Peer-to-Peer (Ad-Hoc) Networking*, is a step-by-step guide to building your own access point using Linux, inexpensive PC hardware, and conventional wireless client cards.

- Chapter 6, *Wide Area Network Saturation*, is about extending your range. It looks at using topographic mapping software to evaluate long distance links, and it also examines the myriad antennas, cables, and connectors you are likely to encounter. It also provides a simple method for calculating the usable range of your gear.

- Chapter 7, *Other Applications*, investigates some really exotic (and useful!) applications of 802.11b. It includes practical pointers for setting up point-to-point links, some simple repeaters, assembling a 2.4GHz antenna from ordinary household objects, and lots of other fun hackery. It also includes an implementation of a dynamic "captive portal" firewall using open source software.

- Chapter 8, *Radio Free Planet*, is a resource guide to some of the major players in the wireless network access revolution. Here you'll find out how people all over the globe are making ubiquitous wireless network access a reality, all in their free time.

- Chapter 9, *Radio Free Sebastopol*, is the (brief) history of my own experiences in setting up public wireless Internet access in Sebastopol, CA (and in meeting directly with the heads of some of the biggest community efforts in the U.S.).

- Finally, the appendix provides a path loss calculation table, a reprint of the FCC Part 15 rules, and some other useful odds and ends.

Typographical Conventions

The following typographical conventions are used in this book:

Italic

> Used to introduce new terms, to indicate URLs, variables or user-defined files and directories, commands, file extensions, filenames, directory or folder names, and UNC pathnames.

`Constant italic`

> Used to show variables for which a context-specific substitution should be made.

 Indicates a tip.

 Indicates a warning.

Comments and Questions

Please address comments and questions about this book to the publisher:

> O'Reilly & Associates, Inc.
> 1005 Gravenstein Highway North
> Sebastopol, CA 95472
> (800) 998-9938 (in the United States or Canada)
> (707) 829-0515 (international/local)
> (707) 829-0104 (fax)

There is a web page for this book, which lists errata, examples, or any additional information. You can access this page at:

> *http://www.oreilly.com/catalog/wirelesscommnet/*

To comment or ask technical questions about this book, send email to:

bookquestions@oreilly.com

For more information about books, conferences, Resource Centers, and the O'Reilly Network, see the O'Reilly web site at:

http://www.oreilly.com

Acknowledgments

I would like to thank the O'Reilly Network Team, my parents, and especially Cat for their endless encouragement and keeping me sane (and, in some cases, even sensible).

Also, my sincere thanks to Schuyler Erle, Adam Flaherty, Nate Boblitt, and Jim Rosenbaum for helping to turn the NoCat idea into an actual living project. Thanks as well to Matt Peterson, Matt Westervelt Adam Shand, Terry Schmidt, and the countless other pioneers of ultra-hyper-connectivity.

Thanks go to the reviewers and read early drafts and made comments: Mike Bertsch, Simson Garfinkel, Justin Lancaster, Nicholas Maddix, and Matt Peterson. Thanks also go to all the people at O'Reilly & Associates who turned this manuscript into a finished book: Sue Miller, my editor; Leanne Soylemez, the production editor; graphic artist Rob Romano; Catherine Morris, copyeditor; and Mary Anne Weeks Mayo, who provided quality control.

CHAPTER 1

Wireless Community Networks

In recent times, the velocity of technology development has exceeded "blur" and is now moving at speeds that defy description. Internet technology in particular has made astounding strides in the last few years. Where only a few short years ago 56Kb modems were all the rage, many tech heads now find themselves complaining about how slow their company's T1 connection seems compared to their 6Mb DSL connection at home.

Never before have so many had free and fast access to so much information. As more people get a taste of millisecond response times and megabit download speeds, they seem only to hunger for more. In most places, the service everyone is itching for is *DSL*, or *Digital Subscriber Line* service. It provides high bandwidth (typically, anywhere from 384Kbps to 6Mbps) over standard copper telephone lines, *if* your installation is within about three miles of the telephone company's CO, or central office (this is a technical constraint of the technology). DSL is generally preferred over cable modems, because a DSL connection provides guaranteed bandwidth (at least to the telephone company) and thus is not directly affected by the traffic habits of everyone else in your neighborhood. It isn't cheap, ranging anywhere from $50 to $300 per month, plus ISP and equipment charges, but that doesn't seem to be discouraging demand.

Telephone companies, of course, are completely enamored with this state of affairs. In fact, the intense demand for high-bandwidth network access has led to so much business that enormous lead times for DSL installations are now the rule in many parts of the country. In many areas, if you live outside the perceived "market" just beyond range of the CO, lead times are sometimes quoted at two to three years (marketing jargon for "never, but we'll take your money anyway, if you like"). Worse than that, in the wake of widespread market consolidation, some customers who were quite happy with their DSL service are finding themselves stranded when their local ISP goes out of business.*

What are the alternatives for people who want high-speed Internet access but aren't willing to wait for companies to package a solution for them? The telephone companies own the copper, and the cable companies own the coax.

Wireless networking now provides easy, inexpensive, high-bandwidth network services for anyone who cares to set it up.

Approved in 1997 by the IEEE Standards Committee, the 802.11 specification detailed the framework necessary for a standard method of wireless networked communications. It uses the 2.4GHz microwave band designated for low-power, unlicensed use by the FCC in the U.S. in 1985. 802.11 provided for network speeds of one or two megabits, using either of two incompatible encoding schemes: Frequency Hopping Spread Spectrum (FHSS) and Direct Sequence Spread Spectrum (DSSS).

In September, 1999, the 802 committee extended the specification, deciding to standardize on DSSS. This extension, 802.11b, allowed for new, more exotic encoding techniques. This pushed up the throughput to a much more respectable 5.5 or 11Mbps. While breaking compatibility with FHSS schemes, the extensions made it possible for new equipment to continue to interoperate with older 802.11 DSSS hardware. The technology was intended to provide "campus" access to network services, offering typical usable ranges of about 1500 feet.

It didn't take long for some sharp hacker types (and, indeed, a few CEO and FCC types) to realize that by using 802.11b client gear in conjunction with standard radio equipment, effective range can extend to more than twenty miles and potentially provide thousands of people with bandwidth reaching DSL speeds, for minimal hardware cost. Connectivity that previously had to creep up monopoly-held wires can now fly in through the walls with significantly higher performance. And since 802.11b uses unlicensed radio spectrum, full-time connections can be set up *without paying a dime in airtime or licensing fees*.

While trumping the telco and cable companies with off-the-shelf magical hardware may be an entertaining fantasy, how well does 802.11b equipment actually perform in the real world? How can it be applied effectively to provide access to the Internet?

---

* One currently circulating meme for this phenomenon deems a stranded DSL customer "North-pointed," in honor of the ISP NorthPoint.net, which went out of business last March, leaving thousands without access.

The Problem

An obvious application for 802.11b is to provide the infamous "last mile" network service. This term refers to the stretch that sits between those who have good access to the Internet (ISPs, telcos, and cable companies) and those who want it (consumers). This sort of arrangement requires 802.11b equipment at both ends of the stretch (for example, at an ISP's site and at a consumer's home).

Unfortunately, the nature of radio communications at microwave frequencies requires *line of sight* for optimal performance. This means that there should be an unobstructed view between the two antennas, preferably with nothing but a valley between them. This is absolutely critical in long distance, low power applications. Radio waves penetrate many common materials, but range is significantly reduced when going through anything but air. Although increasing transmission power can help get through trees and other obstructions, simply adding amplifiers isn't always an option, as the FCC imposes strict limits on power. (See the Appendix for a copy of the FCC Part 15 rules that pertain to 2.4GHz emissions. We will return to this subject in detail in Chapter 7.)

Speaking of amplifiers, a related technical obstacle to wireless nirvana is how to deal with noise in the band. The 2.4GHz band isn't reserved for use solely by 802.11b gear. It has to share the band with many other devices, including cordless phones, wireless X-10 cameras, Bluetooth equipment, burglar alarms, and even microwave ovens! Using amplifiers to try to "blast" one's way through intervening obstacles and above the background noise is the social equivalent of turning your television up to full volume so you can hear it in your front yard (maybe also to hear it above your ringing telephone and barking dog, or even your neighbor's loud television...).

If data is going to flow freely over the air, there has to be a high degree of coordination among those who set it up. As the airwaves are a public resource, the wireless infrastructure should be built in a way that benefits the most people possible, for the lowest cost. How can 802.11b effectively connect people to each other?

How ISPs Are Attempting a Solution

Visions of license-free, monopoly shattering, high-bandwidth networks are certainly dancing through the heads of some business-minded individuals these days. On the surface, it looks like sound reasoning: if people are conditioned into believing that 6Mb DSL costs $250 per month to provide, then they'll certainly be willing to pay at least that much for an 11Mb wireless connection that costs pennies to operate, particularly if it's cleverly packaged as an upgrade to a brand name they already know. The temptation of high profits and low operating costs seems to have once again allowed marketing to give way to good sense. Thus, the wireless DSL phenomenon was born. (Who needs an actual technology when you can market an acronym, anyway?)

In practice, many WISPs* are finding out that it's not as simple as throwing some antennas up and raking in the cash. To start with, true DSL provides a full-duplex, switched line. Most DSL lines are asymmetric, meaning that they allow for a higher download speed at the expense of slower upload speed. This difference is hardly noticeable when most of the network traffic is incoming (i.e., when users are browsing the Web), but it is present. Even with the low-speed upload limitation, a full-duplex line can still upload and download data simultaneously. Would-be wireless providers that build on 802.11b technology are limited to half-duplex, shared bandwidth connections. This means that to provide the same quality of service as a wired DSL line, they would need four radios for each customer: two at each end, using one for upstream and one for downstream service. If the network infrastructure plan is to provide a few (or even a few dozen) wireless access sites throughout a city, these would need to be shared between all of the users, further degrading network performance, much like the cable modem nightmare. Additional access sites could help, but adding equipment also adds to hardware and operating costs.

Speaking of access points, where exactly should they be placed? Naturally, the antennas should be located wherever the greatest expected customer base can see them. Unless you've tried it, I guarantee this is trickier than it sounds. Trees, metal buildings, chain link fences, and the natural lay of the land make antenna placement an interesting challenge for a hobbyist, but a nightmare for a network engineer. As we'll see later, a basic antenna site needs power and a sturdy mast to mount equipment to, and, preferably, it also has access to a wired backbone. Otherwise, even more radio gear is needed to provide network service to the tower.

Suppose that marketing has sufficiently duped would-be customers and claims to have enough tower sites to make network services at least a possibility. Now imagine that a prospective customer actually calls, asking for service. How does the WISP know if service is possible? With DSL, it's straightforward: look up the customer's phone number in the central database, figure out about how far they are from the CO, and give them an

---

* Wireless Internet Service Providers. No, I didn't make that one up.

estimate. Unfortunately, no known database can tell you for certain what a given address has line of sight to.

As we'll see later, topographical software can perform some preliminary work to help rule out at least the definite impossibilities. Some topographical packages even include tree and ground clutter data. At this point, we might even be able to upgrade the potential customer to a "maybe." Ultimately, however, the only way to know if a particular customer can reach the WISP's backbone over wireless is to send out a tech with test gear, and try it.

So now the poor WISP needs an army of technically capable people with vans, on call for new installations, who then need to make on-site calls to people who aren't even customers yet. And if they're lucky, they might even get a test shot to work, at which point equipment can finally be installed, contracts signed, and the customer can get online at something almost resembling DSL. That is, the customer can be online until a bird perches on the antenna, or a new building goes up in the link path, or the leaves come out in the spring and block most of the signal (at which point, I imagine the customer would be referred to the fine print on that contract).

I think you can begin to see exactly where the bottom line is in this sort of arrangement. It's certainly not anyone's fault, but this solution just isn't suited to the problem, because the only entity with enough resources to seriously attempt it would likely be the phone company. What hope does our "wireless everywhere" vision have in light of all of the previously mentioned problems? Perhaps a massively parallel approach would help....

How Cooperatives Are Making It Happen

The difficulties of a commercial approach to wireless access exist because of a single social phenomenon: the customer is purchasing a solution and is therefore expecting a reasonable service for their money. In a commercial venture, the WISP is ultimately responsible for upholding their end of the agreement or otherwise compensating the customer.

The "last mile" problem has a very different outlook if each member of the network is responsible for keeping his own equipment online. Like many ideas whose time has come, the community wireless network phenomenon is unfolding right now, all over the planet.* People who have been fed up

---

* GAWD, the Global Access Wireless Database, lists 198 public wireless access points at the time of this writing. Check out *http://www.shmoo.com/gawd/* to add your own or search for one.

with long lead times and high equipment and installation costs are pooling their resources to provide wireless access to friends, family, neighbors, schools, and remote areas that will likely never see broadband access otherwise. As difficult as the WISP nightmare example has made this idea sound, people everywhere are learning that they don't necessarily need to pay their dues to the telco to make astonishing things happen. They are discovering that it is indeed possible to provide very high bandwidth connections to those who need it for pennies—not hundreds of dollars—a month.

Of course, if people are going to be expected to run a wireless gateway, they need access either to highly technical information or to a solution that is no more difficult than plugging in a connector and flipping a switch. While bringing common experiences together can help find an easy solution more quickly, only a relatively small percentage of people on this planet know that microwave communications are even possible. Even fewer know how to effectively connect a wireless network to the Internet. As we'll see later, ubiquity is critical if wide area wireless access is going to be usable (even to the techno über-elite). It is in *everyone's* best interest to cooperate, share what they know, and help make bandwidth as pervasive as the air we breathe.

The desire to end this separation of "those in the know" from "those who want to know" is helping to bring people away from their computer screens and back into their local neighborhoods. In the last year, dozens of independent local groups have formed with a very similar underlying principle: get as many people as possible connected to each other for the lowest possible cost. Web sites, mailing lists, community meetings, and even IRC channels are being set up to share information about extending wireless network access to those who need it. Wherever possible, ingeniously simple and inexpensive (yet powerful) designs are being drawn up and given away. Thousands of people are working on this problem not for a personal profit motive, but for the benefit of the planet.

It is worth pointing out here that ISPs and telcos are in no way threatened by this technology; in fact, Internet service will be in even greater demand as wireless cooperatives come online. The difference is that many end users will have access without the need to tear down trees and dig up streets, and many others may find that network access in popular areas will be provided gratis, as a community service or on a cooperative trust basis, rather than as a corporate commodity.

About This Book

The ultimate goal of this book is to get you excited about this technology and arm you with the information you need to make it work in your community. We will demonstrate various techniques and equipment for connecting wireless networks to wired networks, and look at how others "in the know" are getting their neighborhoods, schools, and businesses talking to each other over the air. Along the way, we will visit the outer limits of what is possible with 802.11b networking, how to stretch the range to miles and ways of providing access for hundreds. If your budget won't allow for all of the networking gear you need, we'll show you how to build some of your own.

Through the efforts of countless volunteers and hobbyists, more bits are being moved more cheaply and easily than at any other time in history. There is more happening in the wireless world right now than is practical to put down on paper. Get online and find out what others in your area are doing with this technology (extensive online references are provided throughout this book and in the Appendix).

I hope you will find this book a useful and practical tool on your journey toward your own wireless utopia.

CHAPTER 2
Defining Project Scope

What do you want to accomplish? As a sysadmin, this is a question I ask whenever a user comes to me with a new request. It's easy to get wrapped up in implementation details while forgetting exactly what it is you set out to do in the first place. As projects get more complex, it's easy to find yourself "spinning your wheels" without actually getting anywhere.

The most common questions I've encountered about 802.11b networking seem to be the simplest:

- How much does it cost?
- How far will it go?
- Can I use it to [fill in the blank] ?

Of course, these questions have pat theoretical answers, but they all have the same practical answer: "It depends!" It is easiest to explain how people have applied wireless to fit their needs and answer these questions by way of example.

People are using 802.11b networking in three general applications: *point-to-point links*, *point-to-multipoint links*, and *ad-hoc* (or *peer-to-peer*) *workgroups*. A typical point-to-point application would be to provide network bandwidth where there isn't any otherwise available. For example, suppose you have a DSL line at your office but can't get one installed at your house (due to central office distance limits). If you have an unobstructed view of your home from your office, you can probably set up a point-to-point connection to connect the two together. With proper antennas and clear line of sight, reliable point-to-point links in excess of 20 miles are possible (at up to 11Mbps!).

One common way of using wireless in a point-to-multipoint application is to set up an access point at home to let several laptop users simultaneously browse the Internet from wherever they happen to be (the living room couch is a typical example). Whenever several nodes are talking to a single central point of access, this is a point-to-multipoint application. But point-to-multipoint doesn't have to end at home. Suppose you work for a school that has a fast Internet connection run to one building, but other buildings on your campus aren't wired together. Rather than spend thousands getting CAT5 or fiber run between the buildings, you could use an access point in the wired building with a single antenna that all of the other buildings can see. This would allow the entire campus to share the Internet bandwidth for a fraction of the cost of wiring, in a matter of days rather than months.

The last class of networking, ad-hoc (or peer-to-peer), applies whenever an access point isn't available. In peer-to-peer mode, nodes with the same network settings can talk to each other, as long as they are within range. The big benefit of this mode of operations is that even if none of the nodes are in range of a central access point, they can still talk to each other. This is ideal for quickly transferring files between your laptop and a friend's when you are out of range of an access point, for example. In addition, if one of the nodes in range happens to be an Internet gateway, then traffic can be relayed to and from the Internet, just as if it were a conventional access point. In Chapter 5, we'll see a method for using this mode to provide gateway services without the need for expensive access point hardware. In Chapter 7, we'll build on that simple gateway to create a public access wireless gatekeeper, with dynamic firewalling, a captive web portal, user authentication, and real-time traffic shaping.

You can use these modes of operation in conjunction with each other (and with other wired networking techniques) to extend your network as you need it. It is very common, for example, to use a long distance wireless link to provide access to a remote location, and then set up an access point at that end to provide local access.

Hardware Requirements

The total cost of your project is largely dependent on your project goals and how much work you're willing to do yourself. While you can certainly spend tens of thousands of dollars on outdoor, ISP-class equipment, you may find that you can save money (and get more satisfaction) building similar functionality yourself, with cheaper off-the-shelf hardware.

If you simply want to connect your laptop to someone else's 802.11b network, you'll need only a client card and driver software (at this point, compatible cards cost between $50 and $200). Like most equipment, the price typically goes up with added features, such as an external antenna connector, higher output power, a more sensitive radio, and the usual bells and whistles. Once you select a card, find out what the network settings are for the network you want to connect to, and hop on. If you need more range, a small omni-directional antenna (typically $50–$100) can significantly extend the roaming range of your laptop.

If you want to provide wireless network access to other people, you'll need an *access point (AP)*. This has become something of a loaded term and can refer to anything from a low-end "residential gateway" class box (about $200) to high-end, commercial quality, multi-radio equipment ($1000+). They are typically small, standalone boxes that contain at least one radio and another network connection (like Ethernet or a dialup modem). For the rest of this book, we'll use the term access point to refer to any device capable of providing network access to your wireless clients. As we'll see in Chapter 5, this can even be provided by a conventional PC router equipped with a wireless card.

While a radio and an access point can make a simple short range network, you will more than likely want to extend your coverage beyond what is possible out of the box. The most effective way of extending range is to use external antennas. Antennas come in a huge assortment of packages, from small omnidirectional tabletop antennas to large, mast-mounted parabolic dishes. There isn't one "right" antenna for every application; you'll need to choose the antenna that fits your needs (if you're trying to cover just a single building, you may not even need external antennas). Take a look at Chapter 6 for specific antenna descriptions.

Site Survey

The most efficient wireless network consists of a single client talking to a single access point a few feet away with absolutely clear line of sight between them and no other noise on the channel being used (either from other networks or from equipment that shares the 2.4GHz spectrum). Of course, with the possible exception of the home wireless LAN, these ideal conditions simply aren't feasible. All of your users will need to "share the airwaves," and more than likely they won't be able to see the access point from where they are located. Fortunately, 802.11b gear is very tolerant of less than optimal conditions at close range. When planning your network, be sure to look out for the following:

- Objects that absorb microwave signals, such as trees, earth, brick, plaster walls, and people

- Objects that reflect or diffuse signals, such as metal, fences, mylar, pipes, screens, and bodies of water
- Sources of 2.4GHz noise, such as microwave ovens, cordless phones, wireless X-10 automation equipment, and other 802.11b networks

The more you can eliminate from the path between your access points and your clients, the happier you'll be. You won't be able to get rid of all of the previous obstacles, but you should be able to minimize their impact by working around them.

Hot Spots

The IEEE 802.11b specification details 11 possible overlapping frequencies on which communications can take place. Much like the different channels on a cordless phone, changing the channel can help eliminate noise that degrades network performance and can even allow multiple networks to coexist in the same physical space without interfering with each other.

Rather than attempting to set up a single central access point with a high-gain omnidirectional antenna, you will probably find it more effective to set up several low-range, overlapping cells. If you use access point hardware, and all of the APs are connected to the same physical network segment, users can even roam seamlessly between cells. Figure 2-1 shows an example of using multiple APs to cover a large area.

Figure 2-1. Using non-adjacent channels, several APs can cover a large area

As detailed in the specification, 802.11b breaks the available spectrum into 11 overlapping channels, as shown in Table 2-1.

Table 2-1. 802.11b channel frequencies

Channel	Frequency (GHz)
1	2.412
2	2.417
3	2.422
4	2.427
5	2.432
6	2.437
7	2.442
8	2.447
9	2.452
10	2.457
11	2.462

The channels are spread spectrum and actually use 22MHz of signal bandwidth, so adjacent radios will need to be separated by at least five channels to see zero overlap. For example, channels 1, 6, and 11 have no overlap. Neither do 2 and 7, 3 and 8, 4 and 9, or 5 and 10. While you will ideally want to use non-overlapping channels for your access points, in a crowded setting (such as a city apartment building or office park) this is becoming less of an option.

You stand a better chance at saturating your area with usable signals from many low-power cells rather than a single tower with a high-gain antenna. As your individual cells won't need a tremendous range to cover a wide area, you can use lower power (and lower cost) antennas, further limiting the chances of interfering with other gear in the band. For example, you could use as few as three channels (such as 1, 6, and 11) to cover an infinitely large area, with no channel overlap whatsoever.

The worst possible case would involve two separate busy networks trying to occupy the same channel, right next to each other. The further you can get away from this nightmare of collisions, the better. Realistically, a single channel can easily support fifty or more simultaneous users, and a fair amount of channel overlap is tolerable. The radios use the air only when they actually have something to transmit, and they retransmit automatically on error, so heavy congestion feels more or less like ordinary net lag to the end user. The sporadic nature of most network traffic helps to share the air and avoid collisions, like playing cards shuffling together into a pack.

You may have total control over your own access points, but what about your neighbors? How can you tell what channels are in use in your local area?

Potential Coverage Problem Areas

While a spectrum analyzer (and an engineer to operate it) is the ultimate survey tool, such things don't come cheap. Fortunately, you can get a lot of useful information using a good quality client radio and software. Take a look at the tools that come with your wireless gear (Lucent's Site Monitor tool, shown in Figure 2-2, which ships with Orinoco cards, is particularly handy). You should be able to get an overview map of all networks in range and which channels they're using.

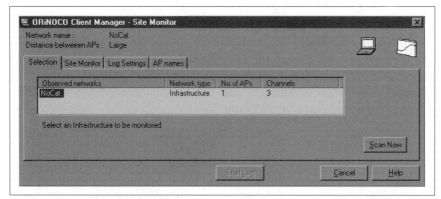

Figure 2-2. Lucent's Site Monitor tool shows you who's using 802.11b in your area

Other (non-802.11b) sources of 2.4GHz radio emissions show up as noise on your signal strength meter. If you encounter a lot of noise on the channel you'd like to use, you can try to minimize it by moving your access point, using a more directional antenna (see Chapter 6), or simply picking a different channel. While you always want to maximize your received signal, it is only usable if the ambient noise is low. The relationship of signal to noise is critical for any kind of communications. It is frequently abbreviated as *SNR*, for signal to noise ratio. As this number increases, so does the likelihood that you'll have reliable communications. (For fine examples of low SNR, kindly consult your local Usenet feed.)

Of course, no known technology can determine the SNR of the actual data you're transmitting or receiving. In the end, you still have to figure out for yourself how to pull signal from the noise once it leaves the Application layer of your network.

To sum up: be a good neighbor, and think about what you're doing before turning on your own gear. The radio spectrum is a public resource and, with a little bit of cooperation, can be used by everyone to gain greater access to network resources.

Topographical Mapping 101

As you roll out wireless equipment, you'll find yourself looking at your environment in a different way. Air conditioning ducts, pipes, microwave ovens, power lines, and other sources of nastiness start leaping into the foreground as you walk around. By the time you've set up a couple of nodes, you will most likely be familiar with every source of noise or reflection in the area you're trying to cover. But what if you want to extend your range, as in a several-mile point-to-point link? Is there a better way to survey the outlying environment than walking the entire route of your link? Maybe.

Topographical surveys have been made (and are constantly being revised) by the USGS in every region of the United States. Topo (short for topographical) maps are available both on paper and on CD-ROM from a variety of sources. If you want to know the lay of the land between two points, the USGS topos are a good starting point.

The paper topo maps are a great resource for getting an overview of the surrounding terrain in your local area. You can use a ruler to quickly gauge the approximate distance between two points and to determine whether there are any obvious obstructions in the path. While they're a great place to start assessing a long link, topographical maps don't provide some critical information: namely, tree and building data. The land may appear to cooperate on paper, but if there's a forest or several tall buildings between your two points, there's not much hope for a direct shot.

The USGS also provides DOQs (or Digital Orthophoto Quadrangles) of actual aerial photography. Unfortunately, freely available versions of DOQs tend to be out of date (frequently 8 to 10 years old), and recent DOQs are not only expensive but also often aren't even available. If you absolutely must have the latest aerial photographs of your local area, the USGS will let you download them for $30 per order and $7.50–$15 per file. You will probably find it cheaper and easier to make an initial estimate with topo maps and then simply go out and try the link.

Interestingly enough, MapQuest (*http://www.mapquest.com*) has recently started providing color aerial photos (in addition to their regular street maps) from GlobeXplorer (*http://www.globexplorer.com*). While there's little indication as to how recent their data is, it may be a good place to get a quick (and free) aerial overview of your local area.

You can buy paper maps from most camping supply stores or browse them online for free at *http://www.topozone.com*. If you're interested in DOQs, go to the USGS directly at *http://earthexplorer.usgs.gov*. We'll take a look at some nifty things you can do with topo maps on CDRom and your GPS in Chapter 6.

## CHAPTER 3

Network Layout

In many ways, 802.11b networking is very much like Ethernet networking. Assuming you want to connect your wireless clients to the Internet, you'll want to provide all of the usual TCP/IP services, such as Domain Name Service (DNS) and Dynamic Host Configuration Protocol (DHCP), that make networking so much fun. To the rest of your network, wireless clients look just like any other Ethernet interface and are treated no differently than the wired printer down the hall. You can route, rewrite, tunnel, fold, spindle, and/or mutilate packets from your wireless clients just as you can with any other network device.

Presumably, no matter how many wireless clients you intend to support, you will eventually need to "hit the wire" in order to access other networks (such as the Internet). How do packets find their way from the unbridled freedom of the airwaves to the established, hyper-interconnected labyrinth of the Internet? This chapter describes what you need to know to do that.

Wireless Infrastructure: Cathedral Versus Bazaar

As with any network supporting different physical mediums, network bridges must exist that are capable of exchanging data between the various network types. A wireless gateway consists of a radio card and a network card (usually Ethernet). In the case of 802.11b, radios participating in the wireless network must operate in one of two modes: *BSS* or *IBSS*.

BSS stands for Basic Service Set. In this operating mode, a piece of hardware called an access point (AP) provides wireless-to-Ethernet bridging. Before gaining access to the wired network, wireless clients must first establish communications with an access point within range. Once the AP has authenticated the wireless client, it allows packets to flow between the client and the attached wired network, effectively acting as a true Layer 2 bridge, as shown in Figure 3-1. A related term, *ESS* (or Extended Service Set), refers to a physical subnet that contains more than one AP. In this sort of arrangement, the APs can communicate with each other to allow authenticated clients to "roam" between them, handing off IP information as the clients move about. Note that (as of this writing) there are no APs that allow roaming across networks separated by a router.

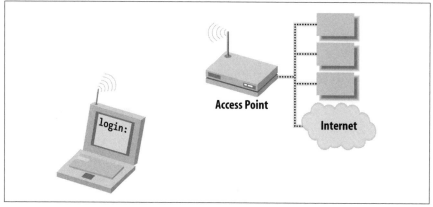

Figure 3-1. In BSS (or ESS) mode, clients must authenticate to a hardware access point before being able to access the wired network

IBSS stands for Independent Basic Service Set and is frequently referred to as ad-hoc or peer-to-peer mode. In this mode, no hardware access point is required. Any network node that is within range of any other can commence communications if they agree on a few basic parameters. If one of those peers also has a wired connection to another network, it can provide access to that network. Figure 3-2 shows a model of an IBSS network.

Note that an 802.11b radio must be set to work in either of these modes but cannot work in both simultaneously. Both modes support shared-key WEP encryption (more on that later).

Access Point Hardware

Access points are widely considered ideal for campus coverage. They provide a single point of entry that can be configured by a central authority. They typically allow for one or two radios per AP, theoretically supporting hundreds of simultaneous wireless users at a time. They must be configured with an ESSID (Extended Service Set ID, also known as the *Network Name* or *WLAN Service Area ID*, depending on who you talk to); it's a simple

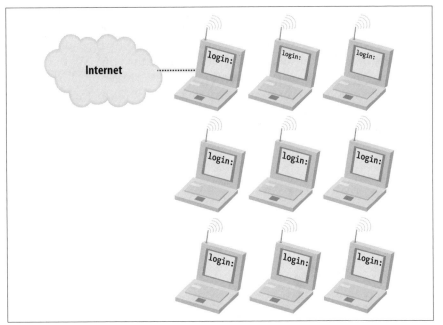

Figure 3-2. In IBSS mode, nodes can talk to any other node in range. A node with another network connection can provide gateway services

string that identifies the wireless network. Many use a client program for configuration and a simple password to protect their network settings.

Most APs also provide enhanced features, such as the following:

- MAC address filtering. A client radio attempting access must have its MAC address listed on an internal table before being permitted to associate with the AP.
- Closed networks. Usually, a client can specify an ESSID of "*ANY*" to associate with any available network. In a closed network, the client must specify the ESSID explicitly, or it can't associate with the AP.
- External antennas.
- Continual link-quality monitoring.
- Extended logging, statistics, and performance reporting.

Other enhanced modes include dynamic WEP key management, public encryption key exchange, channel bonding, and other fun toys. Unfortunately, these extended modes are entirely manufacturer- (and model-) specific, are not covered by any established standard, and do not interoperate with other manufacturer's equipment. It should also be noted that, once a client has associated itself with an AP, there are no further restrictions imposed by the AP on what services the client can access.

APs are an ideal choice for private networks with many wireless clients that exist in a confined physical space, especially on the same physical subnet (like a business or college campus). They provide a high degree of control over who can access the wire, but they are not cheap (the average AP at this writing costs between $800 and $1000).

Another class of access point is occasionally referred to as a *residential gateway*. The Apple AirPort, Orinoco RG-1000, and Linksys WAP11 are popular examples of low-end APs. They are typically much less expensive than their commercial counterparts, costing between $200 and $500. Many have built-in modems, allowing for wireless-to-dialup access (which can be very handy, if Ethernet access isn't available wherever you happen to be). Most even provide Network Address Translation (NAT), DHCP, and bridging services for wireless clients. While they may not support as many simultaneous clients as a high-end AP, they can provide cheap, simple access for many applications. By configuring an inexpensive AP for bridged Ethernet mode, you can have a high degree of control over what individual clients can access on the wired network (see the section "Captive "Catch and Release" Portal" in Chapter 7).

Despite their high cost, APs have their place in building community wireless networks. They are especially well suited to remote repeater locations, due to their ease of configuration, low power consumption (compared to a desktop or laptop PC), and lack of moving parts. We'll go into detail on how to set up an AP in Chapter 4.

Peer-to-Peer Networking

If the goal of your wireless project is to provide public access to network services, the functionality high-end APs provide will almost certainly be overkill, particularly in light of their high cost. Luckily, with IBSS mode, AP hardware is entirely optional.

Radios that are operating in IBSS mode can communicate with each other if they have the same ESSID and WEP settings. As stated earlier, a computer with an 802.11b card and another network connection (usually Ethernet or dialup) can serve as a gateway between the two networks. Add in DHCP and NAT services, and you effectively have a full-blown Internet gateway. As various free operating systems can provide these services and will run well on hardware that many people already have lying around in closets (e.g., 486 laptops and low-end Pentium systems), this mode of operation is an increasingly popular alternative to expensive APs. If you have host hardware available already, the low cost of making a gateway is very attractive (the cost of the average client radio card is $120, or about half that of a low-end AP).

What is missing from a do-it-yourself gateway? Instead of the myriad access control methods that actual APs provide, the only out-of-the-box access control you have available is WEP. As we saw earlier, a shared key does little on its own for security, and it isn't appropriate in a public network setting anyway. So how can we provide network access and still discourage abuse by anonymous wireless clients? See Chapters 5 and 7.

In Chapter 5, we'll build a Linux-based wireless gateway from scratch. In Chapter 7, we'll examine one method of extending the gateway to provide different classes of service, depending on who connects to it.

Vital Services

A network can be as simple as a PPP dialup to an ISP, or as grandiose and baroque as a multinational corporate MegaNet. But every node on a multimillion dollar network in Silicon Valley needs to address the same fundamental questions that a dialup computer must answer: *who am I, where am I going, and how do I get there from here?* In order for wireless clients to easily access a network, the following basic services must be provided.

DHCP

The days of static IP addresses and user-specified network parameters are thankfully far behind us. Using DHCP (Dynamic Host Configuration Protocol), it is possible (and even trivial) to set up a server that responds to client requests for network information. Typically, a DHCP server provides all the information that a client needs to begin routing packets on the network, including the client's own IP address, the default Internet gateway, and the IP addresses of the local DNS servers. The client configuration is ridiculously easy and is, in fact, configured out of the box for DHCP in all modern operating systems.

While a thorough dissection of DHCP is beyond the scope of this book, a brief overview is useful. A typical DHCP session begins when a client boots up, knowing nothing about the network it is attached to except its own hardware MAC address. It broadcasts a packet saying, effectively, "I am here, and this is my MAC address. What is my IP address?" A DHCP server on the same network segment listens for these requests and responds: "Hello MAC address. Here is your IP address, and by the way, here is the IP address to route outgoing packets to, and some DNS servers are over there. Come back in a little while and I'll give you more information." And the client, now armed with a little bit of knowledge, goes about its merry way. This model is shown in Figure 3-3.

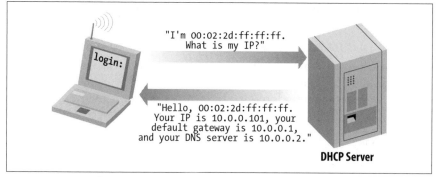

"I'm 00:02:2d:ff:ff:ff.
What is my IP?"

login:

"Hello, 00:02:2d:ff:ff:ff.
Your IP is 10.0.0.101, your
default gateway is 10.0.0.1,
and your DNS server is 10.0.0.2."

DHCP Server

Figure 3-3. DHCP lets a node get its network settings dynamically and easily

In a wireless environment, DHCP is an absolute necessity. There isn't much point in being able to wander around without a cable if you need to manually set the network parameters for whatever network you happen to be in range of. It's much more convenient to let the computers work it out on their own (and let you get back to more important things, like IRC or "Quake III Arena"). Since DHCP lets a node discover information about its network, one can get "online" without any prior knowledge about that particular network's layout. This service demonstrates a condition that network administrators have known for years: users just want to get online without knowing (or even caring) about the underlying network. From their perspective, it should just work. DHCP makes this kind of magic possible.

From a network admin's perspective, the magic isn't even terribly difficult to bring about. As long as you have exactly one DHCP server running on your network segment, your clients can all pull from a pool of available IP addresses. The DHCP server manages the pool on its own, reclaiming addresses that are no longer in use and reassigning them to new clients.

In many cases, a wired network's existing DHCP server serves wireless users with no trouble. It sees the wireless node's DHCP request just as it would any other and responds accordingly. If your wired network isn't already providing DHCP, or if your wireless gateway isn't capable of L2 bridging, don't worry. We'll cover setting up the ISC's *dhcpd* server in Linux in Chapter 5.

DNS

My, how different the online world would be if we talked about sending mail to *rob@208.201.239.36* or got excited about having just been *64.28.67. 150*'d. DNS is the dynamic telephone directory of the Internet, mapping human friendly names (like *oreillynet.com* or *slashdot.org*) to computer friendly numbers (like the dotted quads above). The Internet without DNS is about as much fun and convenient as referring to people by their Social Security numbers.

Much like DHCP, your network's existing DNS servers should be more than adequate to provide name resolution services to your wireless clients. However, depending on your particular wireless application, you may want to get creative with providing additional DNS services. A caching DNS server might be appropriate, to reduce the load on your primary DNS servers (especially if you have a large number of wireless clients). You might even want to run separate DNS for your wireless hosts, so that wireless nodes can easily provide services for each other.

NAT

In order for any machine to be reachable via the Internet, it must be possible to route traffic to it. A central authority, the IANA (Internet Assigned Numbers Authority, *http://www.iana.org*), holds the keys to the Internet. This international body controls how IP addresses are parceled out to the various parts of the world, in an effort to keep every part of the Internet (theoretically) reachable from every other and to prevent the accidental reuse of IP addresses in different parts of the world. Unfortunately, due to the unexpectedly tremendous popularity of the Net, what was thought to be plenty of address space at design time has proven to be woefully inadequate in the real world. With thousands of new users coming online for the first time every day, the general consensus is that there simply aren't enough IP addresses to go around anymore. Most ISPs are increasingly paranoid about the shortage of homesteading space, and they are loath to give out more than one per customer (and, in many cases, they won't even do that anymore, thanks to the wonders of DHCP).

Now we see the inevitable problem: suppose you have a single IP address allocated to you by your ISP, but you want to allow Internet access to a bunch of machines, including your wireless nodes. You certainly don't want to pay exorbitant fees for more address space just to let your nephew get online when he brings his wireless laptop over once a month.

This is where NAT can help you. Truly a mixed blessing, NAT (referred to in some circles as "masquerading") provides a two-way forwarding service between the Internet and another network of computers. A computer providing NAT typically has two network interfaces. One interface is connected to the Internet (where it uses a real live IP address), and the other is attached to an internal network. Machines on the internal network use any of IANA's thoughtfully assigned, reserved IP addresses and route all of their outgoing traffic through the NAT box. When the NAT box receives a packet bound for the Internet, it makes a note of where the packet came from. It then rewrites the packet using its "real" IP address and sends the modified packet out to your ISP (where it winds its way through the rest of the Internet, hopefully arriving at the requested destination). When the response (if any) comes back, the NAT box looks up who made the original request, rewrites the inbound packet, and returns it to the original sender. As far as the rest of the Net is concerned, only the NAT machine is visible. And as far as the internal clients can tell, they're directly connected to the Internet. Figure 3-4 shows a model of a NAT configuration.

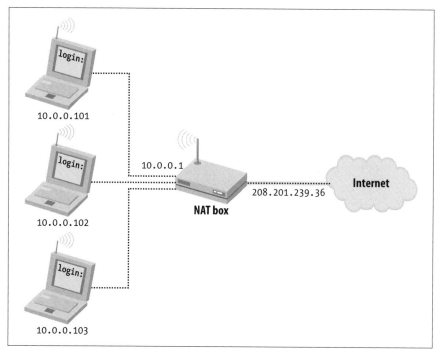

Figure 3-4. Using NAT, several computers can share a single "real" IP address

The IANA has reserved the following sets of IP addresses for private use (as outlined in RFC 1918, *http://rfc.net/rfc1918.html*):

```
10.0.0.0 - 10.255.255.255
172.16.0.0 - 172.31.255.255
192.168.0.0 - 192.168.255.255
```

These are addresses that are guaranteed never to be used on the Internet. As long as your internal machines use IP addresses in any of these three ranges, your traffic will not interfere with any other host on the Net. As an added bonus, since the reserved IP address traffic isn't even routed over the Internet, you effectively get a free firewall for all of your NAT'd hosts.

NAT is handy but isn't without its drawbacks. For example, some services may not work properly with some implementations of NAT. Most notably, active FTP sessions fail on some NAT boxes. Another big disadvantage to NAT is that it effectively makes the Internet a read-only medium, much like television. If you can have only outbound traffic (to web servers, for example) and traffic from the Internet can't reach your machine directly, then you have no way of serving data and contributing back to the Net! This doesn't prevent you from using two-way services like IRC and email, but it does preclude you from easily running services where Internet users connect to you directly (for example, running your own web server from behind a NAT isn't trivial).

Despite these drawbacks, NAT is an invaluable tool for allowing throngs of people to access Internet resources. In Chapter 5, we'll build a Linux gateway that will do NAT for you and handle almost every popular form of Internet traffic you care to throw at it (including active FTP).

Of course, if you're lucky enough to have a ton of live IP address space, feel free to flaunt it and assign live IPs to your wireless clients! Naturally, most people (and, indeed, their laptops) are unprepared for the unbridled adrenaline rush of using a live IP address without a firewall. But if you have that many real IPs to throw around, you must be used to living large. Just don't worry when you find your clients spontaneously rebooting or suddenly serving 0-dAy W@r3z. It's all part of the beautiful online experience.

Security Considerations

Although the differences between tethered and untethered are few, they are significant. For example, everyone has heard of the archetypal "black-hat packet sniffer," a giggling sociopath sitting on your physical Ethernet segment, surreptitiously logging packets for his own nefarious ends. This could be a disgruntled worker, a consultant with a bad attitude, or even (in one legendary case) a competitor with a laptop, time on his hands, and a lot of nerve.* Although switched networks, a reasonable working environment, and conscientious reception staff can go a long way to minimize exposure to the physical wiretapper, the stakes are raised with wireless. Suddenly, one no longer needs physical presence to log data: why bother trying to smuggle equipment onsite when you can crack from your own home or office two blocks away with a high-gain antenna?

---

* As the story goes, a major computer hardware manufacturer once found a new "employee" sitting in a previously unoccupied cube. He had evidently been there for three weeks, plugged into the corporate network and happily logging data before HR got around to asking who he was.

Visions of cigarette smoking, pale skinned über-crackers in darkened rooms aside, there is a point that many admins tend to overlook when designing networks: the whole reason that the network exists is to connect people to each other! Services that are difficult for people to use will simply go unused. You may very well have the most cryptographically sound method on the planet for authenticating a user to the system. You may even have the latest in biometric identification, full winnow and chaff capability, and independently verified and digitally signed content assurance for every individual packet. But if the average user can't simply check her email, it's all for naught. If the road to hell is paved with good intentions, the customs checkpoint must certainly be run by the Overzealous Security Consultant.

The two primary concerns when dealing with wireless clients are these:

- Who is allowed to access network services?
- What services can authorized users access?

As it turns out, with a little planning, these problems can be addressed (or neatly sidestepped) in most real-world cases. In this section, we'll look at ways of designing a network that keeps your data flowing to where it belongs, as quickly and efficiently as possible.

Let's take a look at the tools we have available to put controls on who can access what.

WEP

The 802.11b specification outlines a form of encryption called *wired equivalency privacy*, or *WEP*. By encrypting packets at the MAC layer, only clients who know the "secret key" can associate with an access point or peer-to-peer group. Anyone without the key may be able to see network traffic, but every packet is encrypted.

The specification employs a 40-bit, shared-key RC4 PRNG* algorithm from RSA Data Security. Most cards that talk 802.11b (Agere Orinoco, Cisco Aironet, and Linksys WPC11, to name a few) support this encryption standard.

Although hardware encryption sounds like a good idea, the implementation in 802.11b is far from perfect. First of all, the encryption happens at the link layer, not at the application layer. This means your communications are protected up to the gateway, but no further. Once it hits the wire, your packets are sent in the clear. Worse than that, every other legitimate wireless client who has the key can read your packets with impunity, since the key is

---

* Pseudo-Random Number Generator. It could be worse, but entropy takes time.

shared across all clients. You can try it yourself; simply run *tcpdump* on your laptop and watch your neighbor's packets just fly by, even with WEP enabled.

Some manufacturers (e.g., Agere and Cisco) have implemented their own proprietary extensions to WEP, including 128-bit keys and dynamic key management. Unfortunately, because they are not defined by the 802.11b standard, there is no guarantee that cards from different manufacturers that use these extensions will interoperate (and, generally speaking, they don't).

To throw more kerosene on the burning WEP tire mound, a team of cryptographers at the University of California at Berkeley have identified weaknesses in the way WEP is implemented, effectively making the strength of encryption irrelevant. With all of these problems, why is WEP still supported by manufacturers? And what good is it for building public access networks?

WEP was not designed to be the ultimate "killer" security tool (nor can anything seriously claim to be). Its acronym makes the intention clear: wired equivalency privacy. In other words, the aim behind WEP was to provide no greater protection than you would have when you physically plug into your Ethernet network. (Keep in mind that in a wired Ethernet setting, there is no encryption provided by the protocol at all. That is what application layer security is for; see the tunneling discussion later in this chapter.)

What WEP does provide is an easy, generally effective, interoperable deterrent to unauthorized access. While it is technically feasible for a determined intruder to gain access, it is not only beyond the ability of most users, but usually not worth the time and effort, particularly if you are already giving away public network access!

As we'll see in Chapter 7, one area where WEP is particularly useful is at either end of a long point-to-point backbone link. In this application, unwanted clients could potentially degrade network performance for a large group of people, and WEP can help not only discourage would-be link thieves, but also encourage them to set up more public access gateways.

Routing and Firewalling

The primary security consideration for wireless network access is where to fit it into your existing network. Regardless of your gateway method (AP or DIY) you need to consider what services you want your wireless users to be able to access. Since the primary goal of this book is to describe methods for providing public access to network services (including access to the Internet), I strongly recommend setting up your wireless gateways in the same place you would any public resource: in your network's DMZ or outside your firewall altogether. That way, even in a complete breakdown of security precautions, the worst that any social deviant will end up with is Internet access, and not unrestricted access to your private internal network.

This configuration, as shown in Figure 3-5, leaves virtually no incentive for anyone to try to compromise your gateway, as the only thing to be gained would be greater Internet access. Attacks coming from the wireless interface can easily log MAC address and signal strength information. In IBSS mode, this is an even greater deterrent. As the would-be attacker needs to transmit to carry out an attack, they give away not only a unique identifier (their MAC address), but also their physical location!

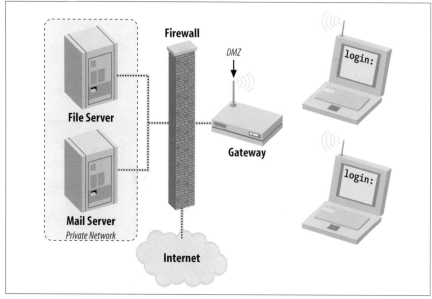

Figure 3-5. Place your wireless gateways outside of your private network!

Assuming that all wireless connectivity takes place outside of your private network, what happens when you or your friends want to connect from the wireless back to the inside network? Won't other wireless users be able to just monitor your traffic and grab passwords and other sensitive information? The next section, "Encrypted Tunnels," addresses this potential problem.

Encrypted Tunnels

Application layer encryption is a critical technology when dealing with untrusted networks (like public-access wireless links, for example). When using an encrypting tunnel, you can secure your communications from eavesdroppers all the way to the other end of the tunnel.

If you're using a tunnel from your laptop to another server, would-be black hats listening to your conversation will have the insurmountable task of cracking strong cryptography. Until someone finds a cheap way to build a quantum computer (and perhaps a cold fusion cell to power it), this activity is generally considered a waste of time. In Figure 3-6, a web server providing 128-bit SSL connections provides plenty of protection, all the way to your wireless laptop. SSL provides application layer encryption.

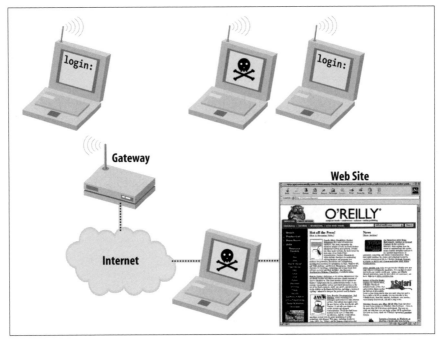

Figure 3-6. WEP only encrypts to the gateway, exposing your traffic to other wireless users and anything after the wire. Tunnels protect your traffic from end to end

SSL is great for securing web traffic, but what about other network services? Take this typical scenario: You're at work or at home, merrily typing away on your wireless laptop. You want to retrieve your email from a mail server with a POP client (Netscape Mail, Eudora, fetchmail, etc.). If you connect to the machine directly, your email client sends your login and password "in the clear." This means that a nefarious individual somewhere between you and your mail server (either elsewhere on your wireless network, or even "on the wire" if you are separated by another network) could be listening and could grab a copy of your information en route. This login could then not only be used to gain unauthorized access to your email, but in many cases also to grant a shell account on your mail server!

To prevent this, you can use the tunneling capabilities of SSH. An SSH tunnel works like this: rather than connecting to the mail server directly, we first establish an SSH connection to the internal network that the mail server lives in (in this case, the wireless gateway). Your SSH client software sets up a port-forwarding mechanism, so that traffic that goes to your laptop's POP port magically gets forwarded over the encrypted tunnel and ends up at the mail server's POP port. You then point your email client to your local POP port, and it thinks it is talking to the remote end (only this time, the entire session is encrypted). Figure 3-7 shows a model of an SSH tunnel in a wireless network.

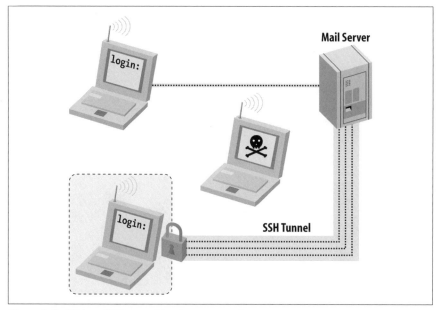

Figure 3-7. With an SSH tunnel in place, your otherwise insecure conversation stays private

With the tunnel in place, anyone who tries to monitor the conversation between your laptop and the mail server gets something resembling line noise. It's a good idea to get in the habit of tunneling anything that you want to keep private, even over wired networks. SSH tunneling doesn't have to stop at POP connections either. Any TCP port (SMTP, for example) can easily be set up to tunnel to another machine running SSH, almost anywhere on the Internet. We'll see an example of how to do that in Chapter 7. For a full discussion of the ins and outs of this very flexible (and freely available) tool, I highly recommend O'Reilly's *SSH: The Definitive Guide*, by Daniel J. Barrett and Richard E. Silverman.

Summary

In order to maintain maximum compatibility with available 802.11b client hardware and yet still provide responsible access to the Internet, we can apply a combination of inexpensive hardware and freely available software to strike an acceptable balance between access and security.

In the following chapters, we'll see how to set up basic wireless access to your existing wired network. We will then build a workable method for providing wireless services to your local community, for minimal cost, while promoting community participation and individual responsibility.

## CHAPTER 4

Using Access Points

As we discussed in Chapter 3, an access point is a piece of hardware that connects your wireless clients to a wired network (and usually on to the Internet from there). As with any piece of bridging hardware, it has at least two network connections and shuffles traffic between them. The wireless interface is typically an onboard radio or an embedded PCMCIA wireless card. The second network interface can be Ethernet, a dialup modem, or even another wireless adapter.

The access point hardware controls access to and from both networks. On the wireless side, most vendors have implemented 802.11b access control methods (like WEP encryption keys, "closed" network ESSIDs, and MAC address filtering). Some have added proprietary extensions to provide additional security, like public key encryption.* Many access points also allow control over what the wired network can send to the wireless clients, through simple firewall rules.

In addition to providing access control, the access point also maintains its own network connections. This includes functions like dialing the phone and connecting to an ISP on demand, or using DHCP on the Ethernet interface to get a network lease. Most access points can provide NAT and DHCP service to the wireless clients, thereby supporting multiple wireless users while only requiring a single IP address from the wire. Some support direct bridging, allowing the wired and wireless networks to exchange data as if they were physically connected together. If the access point has multiple radios, it can bridge them together with the wire, allowing for a very flexible, extendable network.

---

* Unfortunately, as is usually the case with proprietary extensions, these services can be used only if all of your network clients are using hardware from the same vendor.

Another important service provided by APs is the ability to "hand off" clients as they wander between access points. This lets users walk around a college campus, for example, without ever dropping their network connection. Current AP technology only allows roaming between access points on the same physical subnet (that is, APs that aren't separated by a router). Unfortunately, the roaming protocol was left unimplemented in the 802.11 spec, so each manufacturer has implemented their own method. This means that hand-offs between access points of different manufacturers aren't currently possible.

In the last year, at least 20 different access point hardware solutions have hit the consumer market. Low cost models (intended for home or small office use) like the Linksys WAP11 and D-Link DWL-1000AP currently retail for around $200. Higher-end APs like the Orinoco AP-1000 and Cisco Aironet 350 cost over $1000. Typically, higher-priced equipment includes more features, greater range, and generally more stable operations. While every AP will claim 802.11b (or Wi-Fi*) compliance, they are not all alike. Features that set different models apart include:

- Direct bridging to the wired network
- NAT/DHCP service
- Multiple radios (to support more users or for use as a repeater)
- External antenna connectors
- Greater radio output power (most operate at 30mW, while some operate at 100mW or more)

In general, look for an AP in your price range that works for your intended application, with the greatest possible range. Single radio APs can support several users simultaneously, and, as we'll see in Chapter 6, adding APs to your network is probably preferable to adding higher-gain antennas or amps to your existing AP.

Access Point Caveats

One feature that is in high demand (among users trying to go for distance) is the ability to bridge over the air to another access point. Allegedly, the Intel 2011 can do AP-to-AP bridging (as can the Linksys WAP11 after a firmware upgrade). But reports from the field seem to indicate shaky performance at best, as of this writing. Normally, APs don't talk to each other over the air;

---

* Wi-Fi is the "marketing friendly" name picked by the WECA (the Wireless Ethernet Compatibility Alliance) to refer to 802.11b-compliant gear. See *http://www.weca.net* if you're so inclined.

they're designed to talk to client cards. So on a long distance point-to-point link, you'll need to either use a client PC router to talk to an AP or use two routers in IBSS mode (with no AP). See the information in "Point-to-point links" in Chapter 7 if you're interested in long-distance point-to-point links. By the time this book makes it to press, the manufacturers should have their firmware in better shape (we hope).

You should also seriously consider how to fit APs into your existing wired network. Even with WEP encryption and other access control methods in effect, AP security is far from perfect. Because an access point is, by definition, within range of all wireless users, every user associated with your access point can see the traffic of every other user. Unless otherwise protected with application layer encryption, all email, web traffic, and other data is easily readable by anyone running protocol analysis tools such as *tcpdump* or *ethereal*. As we saw in Chapter 3, relying on WEP alone to keep people out of your network may not be enough protection against a determined black hat.

In terms of establishing a community network, access points do provide one absolutely critical service: they are an easy, standard, and inexpensive tool for getting wireless devices connected to a wired network. Once the wireless traffic hits the wire, it can be routed and manipulated just like any other network traffic, but it has to get there first.

Wireless access points that are on the consumer market today were designed to connect a small group of trusted people to a wired network and lock out everyone else. The access control methods implemented in the APs reflect this philosophy, and if that is how you intend to use the gear, it should work very well for you. For example, suppose you want to share wireless network access with your neighbor but not with the rest of the block. You could decide on a mutual private WEP key and private ESSID and keep them a secret between you. Because you presumably trust your neighbor, this arrangement could work for both of you. You could even make a list of all of the radios that you intend to use on the network and limit the access point to only allow them to associate. This would require more administrative overhead, as one of you would have to make changes to the AP each time you wanted to add another device, but it would further limit who could access your wireless network.

While a shared secret WEP key and static table of hardware MAC addresses may be practical for a home or small office, these access control methods don't make sense in a public access setting. If you intend to offer network services to your local area, this "all or nothing" access control method is unusable. As we'll see in Chapter 7, it may be more practical to let everyone associate with your access point and use other methods for identifying users and granting further access. These services take place beyond the AP itself, namely, at a router that the AP is directly connected to (see the captive portal discussion in Chapter 7). Such an arrangement requires a bit more equipment and effort to get started, but it can support hundreds of people across any number of cooperative wireless nodes with very little administrative overhead.

Before we get too fancy, we have to understand how to configure an access point. Let's take a look at how to set up a very popular access point, the Apple AirPort.

The Apple AirPort Base Station

The Mac AirPort is a tremendously popular access point. It looks like a slick, retro-futuristic prop from "War of the Worlds," and it is very portable and rugged. While designed for use with the Mac platform, it works very well as a general purpose access point (and you don't even need a Mac to configure it; see the next section). As I write this, the AirPort sells retail for about $299. What does that get you?

- Direct Ethernet bridging
- DHCP/NAT
- 56K dialup modem port
- User-definable ESSID
- Roaming support
- MAC address filtering
- WEP encryption

What doesn't it get you? It has only one radio (actually, an embedded Orinoco Silver card) and no external antenna connector. But this isn't much of a problem, because the internal Silver card itself has an external connector. See *http://homepage.mac.com/hotapplepi/airport/* or *http://www.wwc.edu/~frohro/Airport/Airport.html* for examples of how to add your own antenna.

Out of the box, the AirPort will try to get a DHCP lease from the Ethernet and start serving NAT and DHCP on the wireless with no password. Yes, by simply plugging your new toy into your LAN, you have eliminated all of the hard work that went into setting up your firewall. Anyone within earshot now has unrestricted wireless access to the network you plugged it into!

While this could be handy as a default configuration (say, at a conference or other public access network), this probably isn't what you want. To change the defaults, you'll need configuration software.

Access Point Management Software

If you have a Mac handy, you are in luck. The AirPort Admin utility that ships with the AirPort is excellent (although only for Mac OS 9 or later). Apple has gone out of their way to make the whole AirPort system easy to set up, even for beginners. If you don't own a Mac, you have a couple of options. It turns out that the innards of the AirPort are virtually identical to the Orinoco RG-1000 (previously, the Lucent Residential Gateway). That means that the RG configuration utility for Linux (called *cliproxy*) also works with the AirPort. You can get a copy of Lucent's *cliproxy* utility at *http://www.wavelan.com*.

Jon Sevy has done extensive work with the AirPort and has released an open source Java client that configures the AirPort and the RG-1000. You can get a copy from *http://edge.mcs.drexel.edu/GICL/people/sevy/airport/*. He has also compiled a tremendous amount of information on the inner workings of the AirPort and has a lot of resources online at this site. Since his utility is open source and cross-platform (and works very well), we'll use it in the following examples.

To use the Java Configurator app, you'll need a copy of the Java Runtime Environment. Download it from *http://java.sun.com/*, if you don't already have it. You can start the utility by running the following in Linux:

```
$ java -jar AirportBaseStationConfig.jar &
```

Or you can start the utility by double-clicking the AirportBaseStationConfig icon in Windows. Figure 4-1 shows an example of the configurator.

The AirPort can be configured over the Ethernet port or over the wireless. When the application window opens, you can click the *Discover Devices* button to auto-locate all of the APs on your network. When you find the IP address of the AP you want to configure, type it into the *Device address* field, and type the password into the *Community name* field. If you're unsure about the IP address or the password, the AirPort ships with a default password of *public* and an IP address of *10.0.1.1* on the wireless interface (it picks up the wired IP address via DHCP; use *Discover Devices* to find it if you're configuring it over the Ethernet). Once you've entered the correct information, click the *Retrieve Settings* button.

The very first thing you should change is the *Community name* on the first panel. Otherwise, anyone can reconfigure your AirPort by using the *public* default! While you're there, you can set the name of the AirPort (which shows up in network scans) and also the location and contact information, if you like. These fields are entirely optional and have no effect on operations.

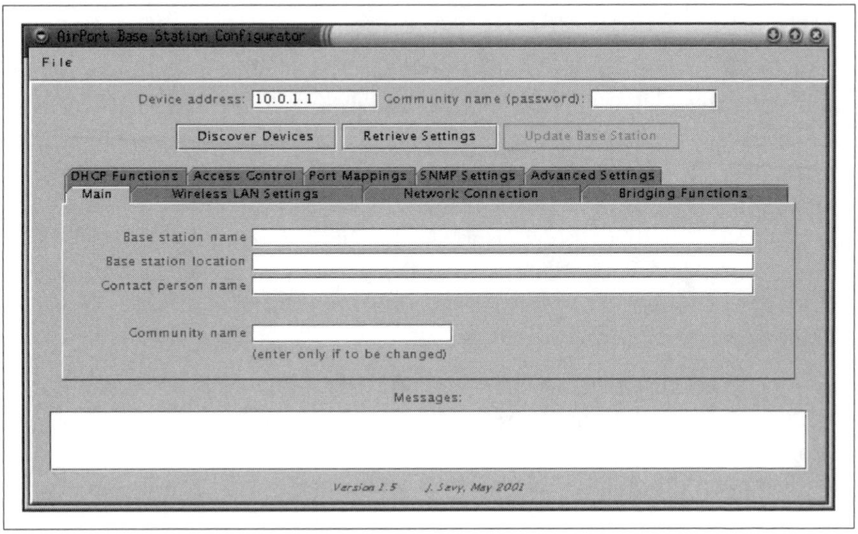

Figure 4-1. The AirPort Java Configurator

You should also choose a *Network name*, under the *Wireless LAN Settings* tab. This is also known as the ESSID, and it will identify your network to clients in range. If you're running a "closed" network, it needs to be known ahead of time by any host attempting to connect, as described in the next section.

Local LAN Access

As stated earlier, the default AirPort configuration enables LAN access by default. If you're using DSL or a cable modem, or if you are installing the AirPort on an existing Ethernet network, this is what you want to use. In the Java Configurator, take a look at the *Network Connection* tab and check the *Connect to network through Ethernet port* radio button.

From here, you can configure the IP address of the AirPort via DHCP, by entering the IP information manually, or by using PPPoE. You'll probably want to use DHCP, unless your ISP requires a manual IP address or PPPoE.

Configuring Dialup

There is also a radio button on the *Network Connection* tab marked *Connect to network through modem*. Use this option if your only network connection is via dialup. Yes, it's very slow, but at least you're wireless. Note that the dialup and Ethernet choices are exclusive and can't be used at the same time.

When you check *Connect to network through modem*, the pane prompts you for phone number, modem init string, and other dialup-related fields. Make sure that *Automatic dialing* is checked, so it dials the phone when you start using the AirPort. Click on the *Username/Password/Login Script* button to enter your login information. On this screen, you can also define a custom login script, if you need to. The default script has worked fine for me with a couple of different ISPs.

Once the AirPort is configured for dialup, it will dial the phone and connect any time it senses Internet traffic on the wireless port. Just start using your wireless card as usual, and, after an initial delay (while it's dialing the phone), you're online.

NAT and DHCP

By default, the AirPort acts as both a NAT server and a DHCP server for your wireless clients.* DHCP service is controlled by the *DHCP Functions* tab. To turn DHCP on, check the *Provide DHCP address delivery to wireless hosts* box. You can specify the range of IPs to issue; by default the AirPort hands out leases between *10.0.1.2* and *10.0.1.50*. You can also set a lease time here. The lease time specifies the lifetime (in seconds) of an issued IP address. After this time expires, the client reconnects to the DHCP server and requests another lease. The default of *0* (or unlimited) is probably fine for most installations, but you may want to set it shorter if you have a large number of clients trying to connect to your AirPort.

If you don't have another DHCP server on your network, the AirPort can provide service for your wired hosts as well. Check the *Distribute addresses on Ethernet port, too* box if you want this functionality.

Only check this box if you don't have another DHCP server on your network! More than one DHCP server on the same subnet is a *bad* thing and will bring the wrath of the sysadmin down upon you. Watching two DHCP servers duke out who gets to serve leases may be fun in your spare time, but it can take down an entire network and leave you wondering where your job went. What were you doing connecting unauthorized gear to the company network, anyway?

---

* If you're just joining us, NAT and DHCP stand for Network Address Translation and Dynamic Host Configuration Protocol, respectively. See Chapter 3 for more details.

If you have more than one AirPort on the same wired network, make sure that you enable DHCP to the wire on only one of them and, again, only if you don't already have a DHCP server.

NAT is very handy if you don't have many IP addresses to spare (and these days, few people do). It also gives your wireless clients some protection from the wired network, as it acts as an effective one-way firewall (see Chapter 3 for the full story of NAT and DHCP). In the Configurator, NAT is set up in the *Bridging Functions* tab. To enable NAT, click the *Provide network address translation (NAT)* radio button. You can either specify your own private address and netmask or leave the default (*10.0.1.1 / 255.255.255.0*).

Bridging

A big disadvantage to running NAT on your wireless hosts is that they become less accessible to your wired hosts. While the wireless users can make connections to any machine on the wire, connecting back through a NAT is difficult (the AirPort provides some basic support for this by allowing for static port mappings, but this is far from convenient). For example, if you are running a Windows client on the wireless, the Network Neighborhood will show other wireless clients only and not any machines on the wire, since NAT effectively hides broadcast traffic (which the Windows SMB protocol relies on). If you already have a DHCP server on your wired network and are running private addresses, the NAT and DHCP functions of the AirPort are redundant and can simply get in the way.

Rather than duplicate effort and make life difficult, you can disable NAT and DHCP and enable bridging to the wire. Turn off DHCP under *DHCP Functions* (as we saw earlier), and check the *Act as transparent bridge (no NAT)* under the *Bridging Functions* tab. When the AirPort is operating in this mode, all traffic destined for your wireless clients that happens on the wire gets broadcast over wireless, and vice versa. This includes broadcast traffic (such as DHCP requests and SMB announcement traffic). Apart from wireless authentication, this makes your AirPort seem completely invisible to the rest of your network.

Once bridging is enabled, you may find it difficult to get the unit back into NAT mode. If it seems unresponsive to the Java Configurator (or Mac AirPort admin utility) while in bridging mode, there are a couple of ways to bring it back.

If you have a Mac, you can do a manual reset. Push the tiny button on the bottom of the AirPort with a paper clip for about two seconds. The green center light on top will change to amber. Connect the Ethernet port on your AirPort to your Mac and run the *admin* utility. The software should let you restore the AirPort to the default settings. You have five minutes to do this before the amber light turns green and reverts to bridged mode.

If you're running Linux, you can easily bring the AirPort back online using Lucent's *cliproxy* utility, without needing a hard reset. Run the following commands from a Linux machine (either on the wire or associated over the wireless):

```
$ cliproxy
[ORiNOCO]> show accesspoints
Searching...

Hostname      Eth Address     IP Address       Description
------------  --------------  ---------------  ---------------------
NoCat         0030.42fa.cade  192.168.0.5      Base Station V3.64

[ORiNOCO]> configure remote 192.168.0.5 public
Config loaded from 192.168.0.5

NoCat> configure terminal

NoCat(config)> no service bridging

NoCat(config)> service napt

NoCat(config)> service dhcp-server

NoCat(config)> done

NoCat> write remote 192.168.0.5 public

NoCat> exit
```

Of course, substitute your password for public and your IP address for the previous sample. At this point, the AirPort should reboot with NAT and DHCP enabled and bridging turned off.

If you're running Windows and need to reset an AirPort in bridged mode, I suggest you make friends with a Mac or Linux user. You might be able to get things back to normal by doing a hard reset (holding down the reset button with a paper clip for 30 seconds while powering the unit up), but I've never been able to make that work. The previous two methods—using a Mac hard reset or the Linux *cliproxy* utility—have worked well for me in the past. I keep a copy of *cliproxy* handy for just this reason.

WEP, MAC Filtering, and Closed Networks

If you really want to lock down your network at the access point, you have the following tools at your disposal: WEP encryption, filtering on MAC address (the radio card's serial number), and running a closed network. The three services are completely separate, so you don't necessarily have to run MAC filtering and a closed network, for example. Combining all these features may not make your network completely safe from a determined miscreant, but it will discourage the vast majority of would-be network hijackers.

To set the WEP keys, click the *Wireless LAN Settings* tab and enter the keys in the fields provided. Also check *Use encryption* and uncheck *Allow unencrypted data* to require WEP on your network. Give a copy of this key to each of your wireless clients.

With MAC filtering enabled, the AirPort keeps an internal table of MAC addresses that are permitted to use the AirPort. Click the *Access Control* tab and enter as many MAC addresses as you like. Only radios using one of the MACs listed here will be allowed to associate with the AirPort. The MAC address of a radio card should be printed on the back of it (a MAC address consists of six hex numbers of the form 12:34:56:ab:cd:ef).

A closed network makes the AirPort refuse connections from radios that don't explicitly set the ESSID, i.e., clients with a blank ESSID or one set to *ANY*. To make your network closed, check the *Closed network* box under *Wireless LAN Settings*.

Remember that without encryption, all traffic is sent in the clear, so anyone within range could potentially read and reuse sensitive information (such as ESSIDs and valid MAC addresses). Even with WEP, every other legitimate user can see this traffic. If you need to restrict access to a user later, you'll need to change the WEP key on every wireless client. But for small groups of trusted users, using these access control methods should discourage all but the most determined black hat without too much hassle.

Roaming

Wireless roaming can be very handy if your network is arranged in a way that you can support it. In order for roaming to be possible, all your APs need to be from the same manufacturer, reside on the same physical wired subnet (i.e., on the same IP network, with no intervening routers), and have the same *Network name* (ESSID).

In the AirPort, roaming is automatically enabled if all of these are true. Make sure that all of your AirPorts have the exact same *Network name* under *Wireless LAN Settings*. If for some reason you want to disable roaming, just give each AirPort a different ESSID.

Channel Spacing

In the 802.11b specification (in the United States), the 2.4GHz spectrum is broken into 11 overlapping channels. Ideally, as you add access points to your network, you want to allow your coverage areas (or *cells*) to overlap slightly, so there are no gaps in coverage. Wherever possible, you should keep a spacing of at least 25MHz (or 5 channels) in adjacent cells, as shown in Figure 4-2. Otherwise, traffic on nearby APs can interfere, degrading performance.

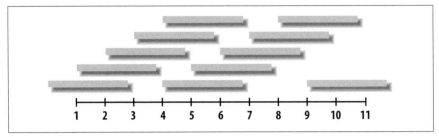

Figure 4-2. Channels need to be separated by at least 25MHz to prevent overlap and possible interference

For example, you may use channels 1, 6, and 11 in an alternating pattern to provide complete coverage without any frequency overlap. Of course, everyone else using 802.11b is trying to do the same thing, and they will probably be using one of these channels. Especially in a crowded area, perfect 25MHz spacing may be impossible. If necessary, you may be able to get away with spacing as close as two or three channels, but don't ever try to run two adjacent networks on the same channel (things may look fine at first, but will fall apart as the network load increases).

To figure out what channels your neighbors use, take a look at your signal strength meter and the other tools that your wireless card came with (the Orinoco card, for example, ships with an excellent *Site Map* utility). You might also check out *NetStumbler*, an excellent network discovery tool for MS Windows. You can get it online for free at *http://www.netstumbler.com*.

CHAPTER 5

Peer-to-Peer (Ad-Hoc) Networking

In traditional wired networks, those responsible for the existence of the network can exert a high degree of control over what happens on their wires. Through border firewalls, proxies, packet filters, and clever routing, the ultimate network content available to an individual node can be manipulated to an almost infinite degree.

The rules are very different when the wires are taken away. Anyone with an 802.11b card can effectively generate whatever sort of packet they like and send it out to anyone within range. As long as nodes can agree on a common method of communications, any number of peer-to-peer networks can be created to exchange data, in a way that makes it prohibitively difficult for a single entity to impose any sort of restriction on the flow of that data.

IBSS mode is one of the most liberating aspects of the 802.11b protocol. It effectively makes expensive access point hardware entirely optional, relying instead on each node of the network to maintain its own communications. Instead of a centralized model, where all clients must be within range of an access point in order to participate, IBSS allows any node to talk to any other node within earshot. If one of those nodes happens to be a gateway to the Internet, it can not only provide access-point–like services but also do the sorts of things that any self-respecting gateway can do: route packets, throttle bandwidth, act as a firewall, etc.

While IBSS refers to a specific mode of 802.11b operations, you will also encounter a couple of other similar (but loaded) terms in your travels: ad-hoc and peer-to-peer. A few vendors have implemented their own "AP-less" mode of operations that, while occasionally providing some interesting features, don't conform to the IEEE standard and will work only with their own hardware. These proprietary modes are referred to in product literature as ad-hoc or peer-to-peer mode. Cards that claim 802.11b compliance may support these additional proprietary modes, but they must also support true IBSS communications.

To further compound the confusion, the Linux wireless tools package calls any non-AP mode ad-hoc and lets you choose which one it uses (IBSS or proprietary) via a system call. In the interest of maximum compatibility, we will be dealing only with true IBSS mode for the rest of the book, and we'll use the terms IBSS, ad-hoc, and peer-to-peer interchangeably (unless otherwise specified).

Building a Wireless Gateway with Linux

To a Linux machine, the wireless card appears to be just another Ethernet device. The wireless driver in the kernel provides a network device (e.g., *eth0*) that can do all of the things any other network device can do. The rest of the system is completely unaware that communications are happening over radio. If you have ever built a firewall with Linux, much of this section should seem familiar to you.

If you haven't built a firewall with Linux, I highly recommend building one with old fashioned Ethernet to get familiar with the process. O'Reilly's *Building Internet Firewalls* covers the specific networking issues involved in much greater detail than I have space for here. Another excellent document to work through is the Firewall and Proxy Server HOWTO at *http://www.linuxdoc.org/HOWTO/Firewall-HOWTO.html*.

Hardware

Most 802.11b cards on the market today are PCMCIA devices. From a design and manufacturing standpoint, this is an excellent idea, because it simplifies the production line and helps keep costs down. At the time of this writing, wireless cards cost anywhere from $75–$200, with the average hovering around $120. Don't be fooled by their small size; these tiny cards are capable of sending a signal several miles with the proper antennas.

Obviously, to set up a machine as a wireless gateway, you need a computer with at least one PCMCIA slot. Although the most common computers that support PCMCIA are laptops, a desktop or rack mount box with a PCMCIA converter card works just fine. Many vendors (Cisco and Agere, for example) are selling PCMCIA to PCI or ISA converters specifically to fit wireless cards into desktop machines.

As long as the chipset on the PCMCIA converter is supported under Linux, and the wireless card itself has Linux drivers, your wireless card should work fine. It isn't absolutely necessary to use an Orinoco wireless card with an Agere converter, for example.

If you have any doubts about whether your hardware is supported under Linux, be sure to consult the current Hardware HOWTO at *http://www.linuxdoc.org/HOWTO/Hardware-HOWTO/*.

It's also worth noting here that there are a bunch of older 802.11 frequency hopping cards floating around. They come in both PCMCIA and ISA/PCI packages and, unfortunately, are *not* 802.11b-compliant. If you want to be able to support 802.11b clients and data rates greater than 2Mbps, these cards will not help you. Always look for the "b" before you buy (there's a reason why the guy at the computer show is running a killer deal on $20 "wireless adapters").

In addition to a PCMCIA slot for the wireless adapter, you'll need an interface that connects to another network. In a laptop, this is usually provided by a network card in the second PCMCIA slot, or possibly a built-in modem for connecting to a dialup account. In a desktop or rack mount machine, any sort of network device can be used, although these days an Ethernet card is probably the most common (second only to dialup).

As far as actual computing hardware goes, you might consider using an older laptop as a gateway. It draws less power than a desktop, has built-in battery backup, and typically gives you two PCMCIA slots to work with. A 486 DX4/100 laptop can easily support several people as a masquerading gateway, as long as it has enough RAM (16 to 32MB should be plenty) and isn't doing anything other than routing packets and providing DHCP. We'll design our gateway to work "headless," so even a working LCD panel won't be a requirement (assuming your laptop has an external video connector to initially configure it). You can often pick up older used laptops at thrift stores or computer surplus stores for under $200 (just be sure to try before you buy; it does need to boot!).

The hard disk space required is a matter of personal preference and how much you want the gateway to do beyond providing access. While a more-than-complete Linux distribution can fill more than 2GB, you can easily squeeze a fully functional gateway into 20MB or less. In the section "Prebuilt Linux Distributions" at the end of this chapter, we'll see some examples of gateway distributions that fit entirely on a single floppy disk (no hard drive required!).

Of course, if you already have a machine on your network providing firewall services, it's a relatively simple matter to install a wireless adapter in it and have it serve as a gateway. If you already have a firewall running Linux, feel free to skip the Linux Distribution section.

For the purposes of example, I'll assume that we're installing an Orinoco Silver card into a laptop with a small hard drive and an Ethernet connection to the Internet.

Linux Distribution

Choosing a distribution (much like choosing an operating system) should be a straightforward process: identify your project goals and requirements, assess what each of the competing choices provides, and make your choice. Unfortunately, the ultimate choice of "which one" seems to be increasingly driven by marketing machinery and passionate treatises on Usenet instead of simple design details.

Rather than settling on a particular Linux distribution (and accidentally revealing my tendency to Slack), here are some components that are absolutely vital to a wireless gateway, and should ideally be provided by your distribution.

These are the mandatory components:

- Linux 2.2 or 2.4 kernel
- Firewall tools (*ipchains* or *iptables*)
- PCMCIA-CS
- Wireless Tools package
- a DHCP server
- Your favorite text editor

These components are optional:

- GCC, for compiling drivers and tools
- PPP, for dialup ISP access
- SSH, for remote administration

Here are things you won't need (and they'd probably just get in the way):

- X Windows, including Gnome, KDE, or any other window manager
- Network services you don't intend to provide on the gateway itself (NFS, Samba, print services, etc.)

Installing Linux is very straightforward with most modern distributions. Typically, simply booting from the CD will get the process going. I'll assume that you have the system installed and running on your existing network for the rest of this section. If you need help getting to your first login: prompt, there are tons of great references on how to install Linux online. You might start with the wealth of information from the Linux Documentation Project at *http://www.linuxdoc.org*.

Kernel Configuration

Once your system software is installed, you'll need to configure the kernel to provide wireless drivers and firewall services. The parameters that need to be set depend on which kernel you're running. The 2.2 kernel has been around for quite a while and has proven itself stable in countless production environments. The 2.4 kernel moved out of pre-release in January 2001 and is up to 2.4.5 as of this writing. While much more rich in features and functionality, it is also a much larger and more complex piece of software. For a new installation on a machine with adequate RAM (at least 16MB for a simple gateway), the 2.4 kernel is probably the best choice, as more and more developers are actively developing drivers for this platform. If space is tight, or you have an existing machine running 2.2 that you would like to turn into a gateway, 2.2 works fine in most cases.

Let's look at the specific kernel parameters that need to be set for each kernel. In either case, first *cd* to */usr/src/linux* and run *make menuconfig*. For these examples, we'll assume you're using either 2.2.19 or 2.4.5. Feel free to compile in any or all of these options as loadable modules, where applicable.

Linux 2.2.19

In addition to drivers specific to your hardware (SCSI or IDE drivers, standard filesystems, etc.), make sure the following parameters are compiled into the kernel:

Under *Loadable module support:*

• Enable loadable module support

Under *Networking options:*

• Packet socket
• Network firewalls
• Socket Filtering
• IP: firewalling
• IP: masquerading
• IP: ICMP masquerading (if you want to use tools like *ping* and *traceroute*)

Under *Network device support:*

- Wireless LAN (non-hamradio)

Note that you need to enable only the Wireless LAN category, not any of the specific drivers. This enables the kernel's wireless extensions and provides the */proc/net/wireless* monitoring interface. Don't worry about PCMCIA network drivers; these will be provided by the PCMCIA-CS package. See the PCMCIA-CS section later in this chapter for details.

Linux 2.4.5

Verify that the following are built into your kernel:

Under *Loadable module support:*

- Enable loadable module support

Under *General setup:*

- Support for hot-pluggable devices

This enables the *PCMCIA/CardBus support* category. Under that section, enable the following:

- PCMCIA/CardBus support.
- CardBus support (only if you have a CardBus network card, i.e., most 100baseT cards).
- Support for your PCMCIA bridge chipset. Most are i82365, although it generally doesn't hurt to compile in both.

Under *Networking options:*

- Packet socket
- Socket Filtering
- TCP/IP networking
- Network packet filtering

This enables the *IP: Netfilter Configuration* category. Under that section, enable the following:

- Connection tracking
- FTP protocol support
- IP tables support
- Packet filtering
- Full NAT
- MASQUERADE target support

Under *Network device support* there are two subcategories of interest. Under *Wireless LAN (non-hamradio)*:

- Wireless LAN (non-hamradio)
- Hermes support (Orinoco/WavelanIEEE/PrismII/Symbol 802.11b card)

Support for Orinoco and other Prism II cards used to be provided by PCM-CIA-CS (as wvlan_cs), but has now moved into the kernel itself (as orinoco_cs). Enable *Hermes support* if you intend to use one of these cards. Why this particular driver resides here and not under *PCMCIA network device support* is something of a mystery.

Speaking of *PCMCIA network device support*, be sure to enable the following:

- PCMCIA network device support
- PCMCIA Wireless LAN
- Any PCMCIA network drivers for your hardware

Beyond the above required components, also include the drivers you need for your specific hardware. If this is your first time building a new kernel, remember to keep things simple at first. The dazzling assortment of kernel options can be confusing, and trying to do too many things at once may lead to conflicts that are difficult to pin down. Just include the minimum functionality you need to get the machine booted and on the network, and worry about adding fancy functionality later. The Linux Documentation Project has some terrific reference and cookbook-style material in the Kernel HOWTO at *http://www.linuxdoc.org/HOWTO/Kernel-HOWTO.html*. RTFM[*] and encourage others to do the same!

PCMCIA-CS

PCMCIA and Card Services provide operating system support for all kinds of credit card–sized devices, including Ethernet and wireless cards. The PCMCIA-CS package is actually made up of two parts, the drivers themselves and the utilities that manage loading and unloading the drivers. The utilities detect when cards are inserted and removed and can give you status information about what has been detected.

Software

If your distribution includes a recent release of PCMCIA-CS, feel free to skip this section. You can tell what version you have installed by running */sbin/*

---

[*] Read The Fine Manual. Thanks to the efforts of volunteer groups like the LDP and thousands of contributors, Linux has become possibly the best-documented operating system on the planet. And where the Fine Manual isn't available, the source is. Read it.

cardmgr -V. I've used 3.1.22 and 3.1.26 successfully. The latest (and recommended) release as of this writing is 3.1.26.

If you need to upgrade your PCMCIA-CS, follow the installation instructions in the package (it comes with a current version of the PCMCIA-HOWTO). When building from source, the package expects you to have your kernel source tree handy, so build your kernel first and then PCMCIA-CS. You can download the latest release at *http://pcmcia-cs.sourceforge.net.*

Configuration

Setting up radio parameters is very straightforward. All of the wireless parameters are set in */etc/pcmcia/wireless.opts.*

Here's an example *wireless.opts*:

```
#
# wireless.opts
#

case "$ADDRESS" in

*,*,*,*)
    INFO="Default configuration"
    ESSID="NoCat"
    MODE="Ad-Hoc"
    RATE="auto"
    ;;

esac
```

You may be thinking, "My God, it's full of stars..." But if you have ever worked with *network.opts*, the syntax is exactly the same. If you haven't, those asterisks allow for tremendous flexibility.

The script is passed a string in *$ADDRESS* that gives details about the card that was inserted, so you can have different entries for different cards. The address-matching syntax is:

```
scheme, socket, instance, MAC address)
```

The *scheme* allows for setting up as many arbitrary profiles as you like. The most common use for schemes is on a client laptop, where you may have different network settings for your office wireless network than for your home network. You can display the current scheme by issuing the *cardctl scheme* command as root, and you can change it by using a command like *cardctl scheme home* or *cardctl scheme office*. Both *wireless.opts* and *network. opts* are scheme-aware, allowing you to change your network and wireless settings quickly with a single command.

The second parameter, *socket*, is the socket number that the PCMCIA card was inserted into. Usually, they start with 0 and go up to the number of PCMCIA slots you have available. To find out which is which, insert a card in one slot and issue the *cardctl status* command.

The third parameter, *instance*, is used for exotic network cards that have more than one interface. I haven't come across one of these, but if you have a network card that has more than one network device in it, use this to set different parameters for each device, starting with 0.

I find the last parameter, MAC *address*, very useful because you can match the setting to a specific MAC address. You can even include wildcards to match a partial MAC address, like this:

```
*,*,*,00:02:2D:*)
```

This would match any recent Lucent card inserted in any slot, in any scheme. Keep in mind that the *wireless.opts* is only called to set radio parameters. Network settings (such as IP address, default gateway, and whether or not to use DHCP) are set in *network.opts*.

For our wireless gateway example, we'll need to set up an Ethernet card and an Orinoco Silver card. Include the above code in your *wireless.opts*. Create entries in your *network.opts* like these:

```
*,0,*,*)
    INFO="Wired network"
    DHCP="y"
    ;;

*,1,*,*)
    INFO="Wireless"
    IPADDR="10.0.0.1"
    NETMASK="255.255.255.0"
    NETWORK="10.0.0.0"
    BROADCAST="10.0.0.255"
    ;;
```

Be sure to put these above any section that starts with *,*,*,*) because it will preempt your specific settings. These settings assume that the wired network will get its IP address via DHCP. You can set DHCP="n" (or just remove the line) and include IP address information (as in the second example) if your ISP uses static IPs. The examples assume that the Ethernet card is in slot 0 and the radio is in slot 1. You could also match on the MAC address of your cards if you want the flexibility to plug either card in either slot, although generally, once your gateway is up and running. you'll want to forget it's even on. See the PCMCIA HOWTO for full details on all the tricky things you can do with *$ADDRESS*.

Wireless Tools

The excellent Wireless Tools package is maintained by Jean Tourrilhes. You can get a copy of it online at *http://www.hpl.hp.com/personal/Jean_Tourrilhes/Linux/Tools.html*. He describes the package as follows:

> The Wireless Extension is a generic API allowing a driver to expose to the user space configuration and statistics specific to common Wireless LANs.

These tools provide a method of controlling the parameters of a wireless card, regardless of what kind of card is installed (assuming that the wireless card driver uses the kernel's wireless extensions). They allow you to set the ESSID, WEP keys, operating mode (BSS or IBSS), channel, power saving modes, and a slew of other options. Simply unpacking the archive and running *make; make install* should copy the binaries to */usr/local/sbin* (see the installation notes in the package for more details). The tools currently bundled in Version 21 are *iwconfig, iwspy, iwlist,* and *iwpriv*. They are absolutely necessary for any Linux gateway or client.

Like its networking counterpart *ifconfig*, the *iwconfig* tool operates on a specific interface and lets you view or change its parameters. You can run it at any time from the command line as root to see what's going on. In addition, PCMCIA-CS calls *iwconfig* when a card is inserted in order to set the initial parameters.

Here's a typical *iwconfig* output:

```
root@entropy:~# iwconfig eth0

eth0      IEEE 802.11-DS  ESSID:"NoCat"  Nickname:"Entropy"
          Mode:Ad-Hoc  Frequency:2.412GHz  Cell: 00:02:2D:FF:00:22
          Bit Rate:11Mb/s   Tx-Power=15 dBm   Sensitivity:1/3
          RTS thr:off   Fragment thr:off
          Encryption key:off
          Power Management:off
          Link Quality:56/92  Signal level:-40 dBm  Noise level:-96 dBm
          Rx invalid nwid:0  invalid crypt:0  invalid misc:0
```

As you can see, *eth0* is a wireless device. The ESSID is set to "NoCat" and WEP encryption is off. For security reasons, the encryption parameter is shown only if *iwconfig* is run by root. If there are any other wireless cards in range with the same parameters set, they can "see" this node and communications can commence exactly as if they were on the same physical piece of wire. Run *man iwconfig* for the full list of parameters. The *iwconfig* binary should be in a common binary path (like */usr/sbin* or */usr/local/sbin*) for PCMCIA-CS to be able to use it.

The other tools allow nifty features like monitoring the relative signal strength of other IBSS nodes, showing available frequencies and encoding bit rates, and even setting internal driver parameters, all from the command line. See the documentation for the full details, and there are more examples in Chapter 7.

For most operations involving a wireless gateway, the *iwconfig* tool provides all the functionality we need to program the wireless card. While you're at Jean Tourrilhes' site, also pick up a copy of *hermes.conf* and copy it to */etc/pcmcia*. It will tell PCMCIA to use the new orinoco_cs driver (rather than the older wvlan_cs) for all compatible radios. See his site documentation for more details.

Masquerading

From the IP Masquerade HOWTO (available at *http://www.linuxdoc.org/HOWTO/IP-Masquerade-HOWTO.html*):

> IP Masq is a form of Network Address Translation or NAT that allows internally connected computers that do not have one or more registered Internet IP addresses to have the ability to communicate to the Internet via your Linux box's single Internet IP address.

IP masquerading makes it almost trivial to give an entire private network access to the Internet, while only using one official, registered IP address.

By configuring the gateway's wired Ethernet to use your ISP-assigned address and enabling masquerading between the wireless and the wire, all of your wireless clients can share the Internet connection, as shown in Figure 5-1. The internal hosts think they're connected directly to the Internet, and there is no need to specially configure any applications (as you would with a traditional proxy server).

As with any form of NAT, masquerading isn't without its drawbacks. For example, the connectivity is one-way by default. Internal hosts can connect to Internet resources, but users from the Internet cannot connect to internal nodes directly.

To configure masquerading for the 2.2.19 kernel, save the following script to */etc/rc.d/rc.firewall*, and add a call to it in your */etc/rc.d/rc.local* startup script:

```
#!/bin/sh

echo "Enabling IP masquerading..."

# Set the default forwarding policy to DENY
/sbin/ipchains -P forward DENY

# Enable masquerading from the local network
/sbin/ipchains -A forward -s 10.0.0.0/24 -j MASQ

# Turn on forwarding in the kernel (required for MASQ)
echo "1" > /proc/sys/net/ipv4/ip_forward
```

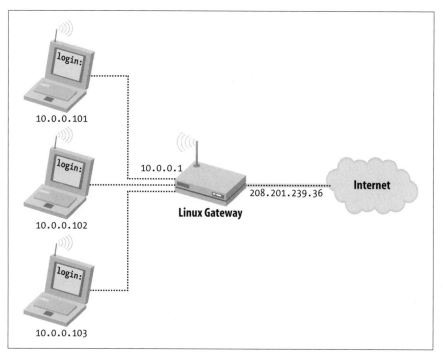

Figure 5-1. Using masquerading, an entire private network can "hide" behind a single real IP address

For Linux 2.4.5, install these commands in the same place, but use *iptables* to set up the masquerading rules:

```
#!/bin/sh

echo "Enabling IP Masquerading..."
/sbin/iptables -t nat -A POSTROUTING -o eth0 -j MASQUERADE

# Turn on forwarding in the kernel (required for MASQ)
echo "1" > /proc/sys/net/ipv4/ip_forward
```

Be sure to substitute *eth0* with the interface name of your wireless card. You can also get a copy of these sample scripts at: *http://www.oreilly.com/catalog/wirelesscommnet/*.

These rules will enable anyone within range of your radio to masquerade behind your live IP address and access the Internet as if they were directly connected.

DHCP Services

As seen in Chapter 3, DHCP lets network clients automatically discover the proper network parameters without human intervention. If we want our wireless clients to use DHCP, we need to provide it on the wireless interface.

 You may be thinking, "Why not just bridge the two networks together and use my network's existing DHCP service?" Unfortunately, many 802.11b manufacturers (including Lucent) recognize that if Layer 2 bridging were possible in their client cards, then there would be very little need for their high-end (and expensive) access points. As a result, the ability to bridge has been specifically disabled in the client card's firmware. Some manufacturers (notably Cisco) still allow bridging at the link layer.

The standard DHCP server was written by the Internet Software Consortium. If it wasn't provided by your distribution, pick up a copy at *http:// www.isc.org/products/DHCP/*. Configuration is very straightforward. Just create an *etc/dhcpd.conf* with the following information:

```
subnet 10.0.0.0 netmask 255.255.255.0 {
    range 10.0.0.100 10.0.0.200;
    option routers 10.0.0.1;
    option domain-name-servers 1.2.3.4;
}
```

Substitute 1.2.3.4 with your local DNS server.

Once that is in place, add an entry in your *etc/rc.d/rc.local* script to call *dhcpd* on the wireless interface. Assuming your wireless card is at *eth0*, this should do it:

```
echo "Starting dhcpd..."
/usr/sbin/dhcpd eth0
```

If *dhcpd* complains about a missing *dhcp.leases* file, try *touch /var/state/dhcp/ dhcpd.leases* as root, and start it again. See the documentation for more troubleshooting techniques and examples, including setting up static leases, WINS servers, groups, and all sorts of things you probably never thought a DHCP server could be capable of.

 Make sure you run *dhcpd* on your wireless interface and not on the wire! Since DHCP is a broadcast protocol, a network can have at most one DHCP server. More than one can cause all sorts of network nastiness as the two duke it out each time a client requests a DHCP lease.

There aren't many free alternatives available to the standard ISC *dhcpd*. One interesting package has been put out by Moreton Bay, an embedded systems manufacturer. They have released their *dhcpd* package under the GPL. While it doesn't have nearly the bells, whistles, and vibra-slaps (*http://www.helixmusic.com.au/vibraslap.htm*) of the ISC's implementation, it does provide simple DHCP service very, very quickly. You can get a copy at *http://www.moretonbay.com/dhcpd/*. The configuration is a little obtuse (it is obviously designed to run in an embedded environment, as it uses tiny binary configuration files).

Security

The examples shown earlier create a simple, open gateway configuration. If you don't care who associates with your gateway (and uses your network), the previous configuration should work fine for you. An example of such a public-access service would be at a conference or user group meeting, where many clients will be connecting to the network, and ease of connection is the primary concern.

In other circumstances, you may not want to allow just any stranger to use your network. Suppose you wanted a wireless gateway for your network at home, and you set up the gateway to use your DSL line's external IP address. Anyone who was within range of your radio could potentially connect, drain your bandwidth, and even send spam or attack other machines on the network. All of this traffic would originate from your IP address, which you are contractually (not to mention socially) responsible for.

If you want to simply allow access for yourself and your friends, enabling WEP encryption can serve as an easy and effective deterrent to would-be network hijackers. When using a WEP, all clients that want to talk to each other must use the same key. In most clients, it can be specified as either a hexadecimal number or as an ASCII string. The length of the key depends on the level of encryption you want to use. As the 802.11b spec allows for 40-bit keys, using it will allow any kind of hardware that complies with the specification to communicate with each other. Some manufacturers have released their own 128-bit encryption implementations, but because it isn't part of the current standard, such cards will work only with equipment of the same manufacturer.

I highly recommend using 40-bit encryption for simple access control, as it will cause fewer compatibility issues later. (Look into the various recent reports on the validity of the WEP implementation; simply adding more bits to a key doesn't necessarily do much for greater security.)[*]

To use 40-bit keys in Linux, specify either a 5-character string or a 10-digit hexadecimal number as the *enc* parameter to *iwconfig*. Many people like to use strings because they're easier to remember. If you do use an ASCII string, you need to preface it with *s:* to tell iwconfig that a string follows. If you want to set the key to the ASCII string pLan9, you could use either of these two commands:

```
root@gateway# iwconfig eth0 enc s:pLan9
root@gateway# iwconfig eth0 enc 704C-616E-39
```

Note that when using ASCII keys, the key is case sensitive.

To enable WEP on your gateway at boot time, edit your */etc/pcmcia/wireless. opts* to add a *KEY=* line to your wireless section, like this:

```
KEY="s:pLan9"
```

Remember that when making changes to files in */etc/pcmcia/*, it is necessary to stop and start pcmcia services (or reboot) before the changes become active. See the earlier section "PCMCIA-CS" for full details on how to set up *wireless.opts*.

Once your gateway is set up, give your private key to all of the wireless clients that you want to give access to. As long as the ESSID and WEP keys match, you can have a private network that provides Internet access. Other radios in the area cannot use your gateway without this information.

If your intent is to offer network access to your local area without exposing yourself to risk or giving away all of your bandwidth, take a look at the "Catch and Release" Portal in Chapter 7.

Putting It All Together

To recap everything that goes into building the gateway:

1. Install the hardware.
2. Configure the kernel.
3. Upgrade PCMCIA-CS, if needed.
4. Install Wireless Tools.
5. Check */etc/pcmcia/wireless.opts* and *network.opts*, setting the ESSID, network parameters, and WEP keys (if needed).

---

[*] At least four papers on WEP vulnerabilities are making the rounds. They are available online at *http://www.isaac.cs.berkeley.edu/isaac/wep-faq.html*, *http://www.cs.umd.edu/~waa/wireless.pdf*, *http://www.cs.rice.edu/~astubble/wep/*, and *http://www.crypto.com/papers/others/rc4_ksaproc.ps*.

6. Set up firewalling rules for masquerading.

7. Set up *dhcpd* to start at boot.

Once all of that is in place, reboot the gateway to be sure everything initializes properly without human intervention. Congratulations, you now have a wireless gateway!

Prebuilt Linux Distributions

Now that we've gone through all of the effort of building our own wireless gateway, you may be interested to know that others have not only already done it but are also giving away the fruits of their efforts. The big advantage to squeezing a minimal Linux install with wireless drivers onto a floppy is portability; with a floppy disk, you can turn any handy laptop into a wireless gateway. Of course, they lack the flexibility of a full Linux installation, but they can be very handy in a pinch.

Check out these gateway-on-a-floppy distributions:

The Linux Router Project (LRP)
> One of the first Linux distributions on a floppy disk, now with wireless network drivers: *http://lrp.c0wz.com*

The Wireless Router Project (WRP)
> Originally based on LRP, since rewritten and optimized for making wireless gateways: *http://www.nocat.net*

CHAPTER 6
Wide Area Network Saturation

You have an access point. Your laptop is humming merrily along. While working at home or the office is more flexible than ever, you find yourself wondering what it would take to get a signal across the street, at your favorite coffee shop.

Or maybe you live in an area where you're on the perpetual "we'll get back to you" list for broadband services like DSL and cable modems, and you're ready to make it happen now. With the right equipment, enough participants, and the cooperation of the lay of the land, you can make broadband Internet access a reality in your neck of the woods.

Whatever your motivations, you are looking for a way to extend 802.11b beyond the listed 300-meter limit. This is not only possible and completely legal, it's also a lot of fun. You first need to figure out what your target coverage area is, and what resources you need to make it happen.

While extending your private network an extra block or two (or even several miles, with the proper antennas) may be interesting for you, it does nothing for those around you except generate more noise in the band. Most people will find it prohibitively expensive to rent tower space and set up network access for themselves, for wherever they happen to be in town. This has led to the fascinating phenomenon of the cooperative wireless network.

The single best piece of advice I can give you on your journey to the ultimate network (whether public or private) is to fight the urge to blindly go it alone. Get people from your local neighborhood involved. Call a general meeting of interested parties. Find other people in your area who have similar goals, and get your resources together. If there aren't any, join the development lists of any of the major community network groups (see the Appendix) and ask around. Chances are, others have done (or are contemplating doing) what you want to do, and they'll probably be more than happy to share their experiences.

As the number of people interested in wireless network access increases, a public access network stands to benefit from access to more vantage points, both figurative and physical. While you might not have direct line of sight to a place you want to talk to, your neighbor might. And for complimentary network access, they might just be willing to let you install some equipment and use their house as a repeater. Wireless bandwidth costs only electricity and equipment, not telephone or cable company charges. This kind of massively parallel, cooperative arrangement is what makes a high speed wireless wide area network possible. However, I can only give you the technical details; the social details are left as an exercise to the reader.

Topo Maps 102: Dealing with Geographical Diversity

If you want to stretch your signal farther than just across the street, you're going to have to consider exactly what lies between the points of your network. In Chapter 2, we looked at using USGS topographic maps and DOQs to estimate how the land lies between two arbitrary points. In addition to paper and online topographic maps, CD-ROM versions have been around for a few years. While typically geared toward hikers and outdoor enthusiasts, they have a lot to offer the aspiring wide area network engineer.

Software

I have evaluated two popular commercial topo packages, Topo! by National Geographic, and DeLorme's TopoUSA 2.0. Figure 6-1 shows a Topo! rendering of Sebastopol, California. While they're both packed with features, only a few are directly applicable to helping analyze land between two points.

Here are some points to keep in mind when evaluating topo software for link analysis:

- The software should provide cross-section views of a route or drawn trail. This is probably the feature used most often in trying to figure out if the land will cooperate (see the next section for examples).

- Almost any self-respecting topo software package includes the ability to mark up the maps with points and text. The ability to import lat/lon data and translate them into data points is handy if you know a site only by its latitude and longitude.

- If you intend to use a GPS with your software (see the next section), make sure your topo software supports your GPS hardware. Both packages I evaluated support most popular GPS hardware and the NMEA data standard (which virtually all modern GPS receivers speak).

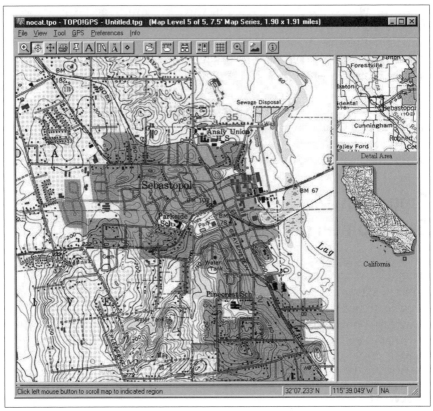

Figure 6-1. A Topo! rendering of Sebastopol, CA

- Both packages I currently use are for Windows only. There are lots of Linux mapping packages floating about that render USGS DOQs and DEMs, but, like a lot of Linux software, it may take a bit of fiddling to get them going. Check out the mapping resource links at the major community wireless sites (see the Appendix), as this is an area of rapid development in the open source community.

Whatever software you choose, it should make it easy to weed out, at a glance, the obviously impossible direct links. If you get a "maybe" (which is frequently the case), you'll just have to go out and try it. Of course, for most of us, that's the fun part.

Using a GPS to Log Prospective Lat/Lon/Alt

Whenever I visit a potential node site, I bring my GPS with me. It logs not only the (more or less) precise latitude and longitude, but also the altitude of the site. This is data you can estimate with a topo map, but it can be handy to have a precise measurement (particularly if you have logged several points in your intended network path). Figure 6-2 shows the use of GPS to tag potential sites.

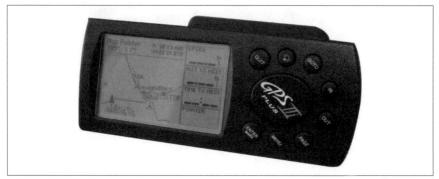

Figure 6-2. You can use a GPS to tag potential sites and analyze them later in software

After collecting points, you can pull them into your topo software and plot them. Draw routes between them to figure out how the land lies between the two points. Figure 6-3 shows a Topo! rendering of a site. Based on this representation, the shot should be a piece of cake.

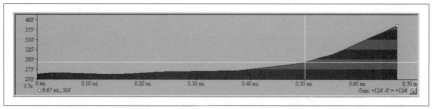

Figure 6-3. Good topo software should be able to give you a cross-section lay of the land between any two points

Keep in mind that, although the topo software has surveyed geological data, it won't have tree or building information. You can get a general idea of how cluttered an area is, but you won't really know until you try the shot. Using the overhead view in conjunction with the cross section, you can not only weed out the obvious negatives, but also find potential work-arounds. Figure 6-4 shows a site that wouldn't work. Maybe you can go around it? Who lives on that hill, anyway?

Using the overhead view to locate key repeater points can be fun. Find out where the good sites are, and try contacting the people at those points. More often than not, people are willing to work with local community groups to provide free access (particularly if they don't have to do much besides provide electricity, and they can get free high-speed access besides).

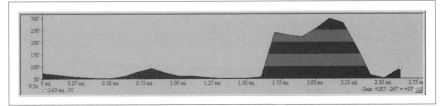

Figure 6-4. This cross-section shows the long distance nightmare: no chance

Plotting the Points on a 3-D Map

DeLorme has the interesting ability to create 3-D renderings of a topo region, complete with data markers and labels; Figure 6-5 shows a rendering. While it's a really cool feature (and very catchy in presentations), it has limited practical value beyond helping to visualize the surrounding terrain. Of course, if you have a whole bunch of data points, it can make for an impressive visual presentation.

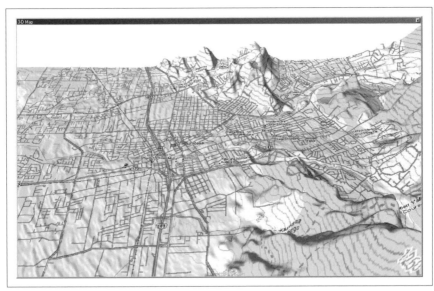

Figure 6-5. DeLorme's TopoUSA gives you a 3-D rendering of any topo region, complete with data points

Once your points are plotted on a map, you can very quickly determine which sites are worth developing. If you can't get direct line of sight to a place you'd like, take a look at the surrounding geography and see if you can find another way. If you can't go through, you'll have to go over or around. Software topo maps can make finding the "bank shots" much easier.

Antenna Characteristics
and Placement

While I am not a radio frequency (RF) engineer, I have had a lot of practical experience setting up 802.11b networks. There isn't nearly enough room here for a full examination of the nuances of radio frequency communications. For more authoritative sources, be sure to check out the great resources in the Appendix—notably, the fantastic publications put out by the American Radio Relay League (AARL), an association of amateur radio operators. Radio is an entire field of study unto itself.

Antenna selection has a tremendous impact on the range and usability of your wireless network. Ironically, the design of almost every external 802.11b card puts the antenna in the worst possible orientation: sideways and very close to the laptop (or desktop). In this position, the radiation pattern is almost straight up and down! Not only does this drive half your signal into the table, it leaves your poor, underpowered radio susceptible to interference from the computer itself.

The one notable exception to this state of affairs is Apple's built-in AirPort card. They've thought enough to include an internal antenna connector that runs up the LCD panel. This is an excellent design with much better range, although it does preclude adding an external antenna. It looks like IBM is the first to play copycat with their i Series ThinkPads as well.

You will see a tremendous difference in signal strength by attaching a small omnidirectional external antenna to your client card and orienting it properly. Which way is properly? That depends on your environment. Try every possible position, with your signal strength meter open. I've put mine on top of my monitor, below the desk, sideways, on the table behind me, and even slung over my shoulder. The best orientation of your antenna is always in the position in which it receives the best signal, so don't be afraid to move the antenna around.

If you're in a pinch without an external antenna, you can watch the wonders of RF by opening up your strength meter and tilting your laptop sideways. Watch that signal bar grow. Go for the green! Learn to type sideways! Better yet, redesign your network to extend your range, and always pack a spare external antenna.

Before looking at adding antennas to your network, make sure your card can take an external antenna. Many low-priced cards don't include external connectors anymore. You will have trouble finding a connector to fit the ones that do, as every manufacturer provides its own proprietary connector (see

Figure 6-6). Check out your friendly local radio supplier for proprietary-to-standard adapters, although they tend to be overpriced.

Figure 6-6. The infamous Lucent Pigtail adapter, list price $80

Of course, if you have good tools and moderate soldering skill, you may have luck making your own adapter, similar to the one shown in Figure 6-7. Why spend $80 on a ridiculous proprietary connector when you can make your own in a few minutes?

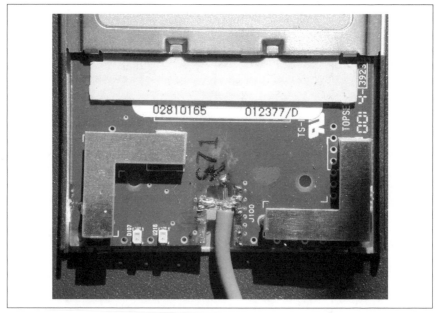

Figure 6-7. A do-it-yourself adapter: $3

The hack-it-in approach is really only practical for a fixed, point-to-point link, as there is no strain relief on the joint. As time marches on, bulk discounts for proprietary-to-standard pigtails are becoming more common.

You shouldn't have to spend more than $20–30 per adapter if you can buy in quantity from a third party. Remember to buy the shortest cable you can use to minimize signal loss in the cable (see the discussion later in this chapter on choosing cable).

Pigtails are manufacturer- (and even model number-) specific, so be sure that you are getting the correct pigtail for the card you intend to use it with. Also, because PCMCIA cards have limited space for connectors, the pigtail plugs tend to be tiny and *very* fragile. One good tug will ruin your pigtail, connector, or both. You have been warned! (Not that I would personally know how easy they are to break. Not even at 2:00 A.M. after too much espresso and too many hours staring at the screen, trying to make a deadline. No sir.)

However you attach your antenna to your radio, always look for a way to position your equipment so it can see the antenna at the other end. This is called having *line of sight* (*LOS*) to the other node. While it helps on short links (such as from your laptop to your access point), it is absolutely critical on long-distance point-to-point links. The ideal path between two antennas would be on towers well above any ground clutter, with a valley in between, pointed directly at each other. This is hardly ever the case, but try to get as close to this ideal as possible.

For outdoor applications, trees are probably going to be your single biggest signal killer (followed by metal, wet masonry, and other 2.4GHz gear). When choosing a place to locate your antenna, consider how changes in the environment will affect your link (what looks like the perfect place in the winter may be completely obscured by leaves in the spring!). Walk around the space you have available, and try to find the best possible place for the antenna. Don't just assume that the highest point is the place to install it. After trying every spot on my roof (in vain) to find line of sight to O'Reilly, I got down and sat on my front porch in frustration. It was then that I noticed that I could see the building, about half a mile away, with nothing in between. Setting the antenna on a tripod on my porch, I instantly got a solid signal. Lesson learned: the right place for the antenna is different in every installation.

Antennas

Antennas do *not* give you more signal than you started with (that's what amplifiers are for). What they do is focus the available signal in a particular direction, like turning the focus head of a flashlight. It doesn't make the bulb any brighter, it just focuses what you have into a tighter space. Focusing a flashlight gives you a brighter beam that covers a smaller total area, and, likewise, more directional antennas give you a stronger perceived signal in a smaller area. All antennas are somewhat directional, and the measure of their directionality is referred to as *gain*. Typically, the higher the gain, the better the range (in the direction that the antenna radiates best in).

There are four different general types of antennas suitable for 2.4GHz use. Each works well for its own application, and no single antenna works best for every application. Plan ahead of time what your goals are, and configure your network to meet those goals. The following sections describe the most common types of antennas, listed in rough order of increasing directionality.

Omni

Omnidirectionals (or omnis), shown in Figure 6-8, radiate outward in all horizontal directions roughly equally. Imagine putting an enormous donut around the center pole of an omni. That is what the radiation pattern looks like. These are good for covering a large area where you don't know which direction your clients might come from. The downside is that they also receive noise from every direction, so they typically aren't as efficient as more directional antennas.

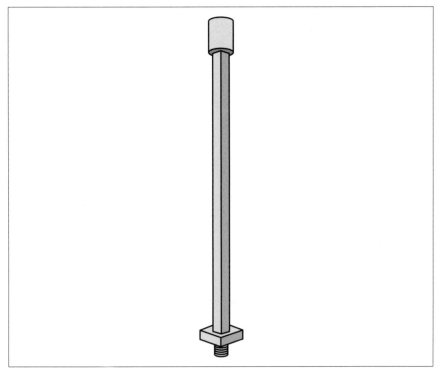

Figure 6-8. Omnis range from tiny extenders to building-mounted poles

They look like tall, thin poles, anywhere from one to five feet long, and they tend to be expensive. The longer they are, the more elements they have (and usually more gain and higher price). They are mounted vertically, like a popsicle stick reaching skyward. They gain in the horizontal, at the expense of the vertical. This means that the worst place to be in relation to an omni is directly beneath (or above) it. The vertical response improves dramatically as you move away from the antenna.

Sector

Picture an omni with a mirror behind it, and you'll have the radiation pattern of a sector (or sectoral) antenna. Sectors radiate in one direction, with a beam as wide as 180 degrees, or as narrow as 60 degrees (or even less). They excel in point-to-multipoint applications, where several clients access the wireless network from the same direction.

Sector antennas (shown in Figure 6-9) come in a variety of packages, from flattened omnis (tall, thin, and rectangular) to small, flat squares or circles. Some are only eight inches across and mount flat against a vertical wall or on a swivel mount. They can also be ceiling mounted to provide access to a single room, like a meeting room, classroom, or tradeshow floor. As with omnis, cost is usually proportional to gain.

Yagi

A yagi looks like an old television aerial. It is either a flat piece of metal with a bunch of horizontal crosspieces or a long pipe with bunch of washers along its length (see Figure 6-10). The typical beam width can vary from 15 degrees to as much as 60, depending on the type of antenna. As with omnis, adding more elements means more gain, a longer antenna, and higher cost.

Some yagis are simply bare, like a flat Christmas tree pointed vaguely in the direction of communications. Others are mounted in long, horizontal PVC cans. They can work well in point-to-point or point-to-multipoint applications, and usually they can achieve higher gain than sectors.

Parabolic dish

In some ways, a dish is the opposite of an omni. Rather than trying to cover the entire area, a dish focuses on a very tight space (see Figure 6-11). Dishes typically have the highest gain and most directionality of any antenna. They are ideal for a point-to-point link and nearly useless for anything else.

Dishes can be solid or mesh, as small as 18 inches across or as big as you like (a 30-foot dish is possible, but probably not very convenient). A dish that can send an 802.11b signal more than 20 miles can be as small as a few feet

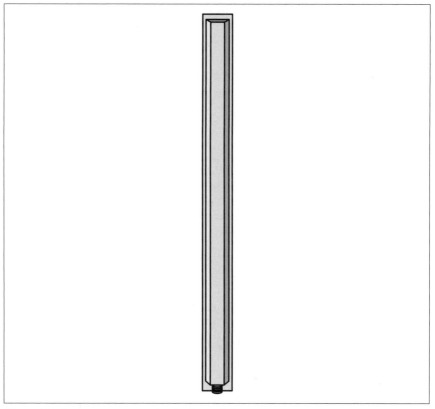

Figure 6-9. Sector antennas tend to be flat and thin

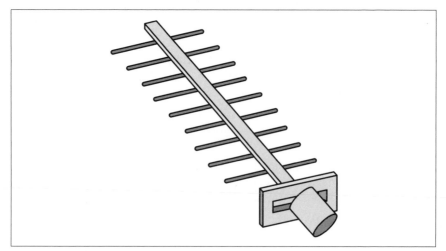

Figure 6-10. A Yagis come in various shapes, but all have multiple elements

Figure 6-11. A 24dB parabolic dish

across. In terms of gain for the buck, dishes are probably the cheapest type of antenna. Some people have been successful in converting old satellite and DSS dishes into 2.4GHz dishes; see the Appendix for links.

One other property of antennas worth mentioning here is *polarization*. The polarization of an antenna refers to the direction that the electrical part of the electromagnetic wave travels in. Both horizontal and vertical polarizations are common, but in some exotic antennas, circular (clockwise or counterclockwise) polarization is possible. The polarization of the antenna on each end of a link must match, or the radios will have trouble talking to each other. Omnis and sectors are vertically polarized. Yagis and dishes can be mounted vertically or horizontally, depending on the application. On a point-to-point link, try both and see which incurs the lowest noise. The polarization of a dish is indicated by the position of the receiving element, not the rear reflector (so an oval dish that goes up and down is probably mounted in horizontal polarization and, therefore, won't be able to talk very well to an omni).

You can also use polarization to your advantage. For example, you can run two parallel links on the same channel, one with vertical and one with horizontal polarization. If separated by a few feet, two dishes can operate quite happily on the same channel without interfering with each other, providing twice the bandwidth on the same frequency. This setup would require four antennas, four radios, and Ethernet channel bonding on each end, but it is entirely possible.

Cabling

Not all coaxial cable is appropriate for 2.4GHz use. The same piece of cable that delivers high quality video and audio to your TV is nearly useless for connecting microwave antennas. Choosing the proper type and length of cable is just as important as choosing the right antenna for the job. A 12dB sector antenna is useless if you lose 18dB in the cable that connects it to the radio. While all cable introduces some loss as signal travels through it, some types of cable do better than others at 2.4GHz.

LMR is a kind of coax cable made by Times Microwave Systems (*http:// www.timesmicrowave.com*) and is possibly the most popular type of cable used for extending 802.11b networks. LMR uses a braided outer shield and solid center conductor, and it comes in various sizes.

Heliax is another kind of microwave cabling made by Andrew Corporation (*http://www.andrew.com*). It is made of a semirigid corrugated outer shell (a sort of flexible copper tubing), rather than the braided strands found in coax. The center conductor can be either solid or a corrugated tube inner conductor. It is designed to handle loads much greater than (legal) 802.11b installations, but it is very expensive and difficult to work with. It is also extremely low loss. The foam dielectric type part numbers start with LDF.*

In addition to Times Microwave's and Andrew's offerings, Belden, Inc., (*http://www.belden.com*) also makes a very common piece of cable that works fine in the 2.4GHz range. You'll frequently see references to 9913; this refers to Belden 9913.

Generally speaking, the thicker and better built the cable, the lower the loss and the higher the cost (see Table 6-1). Cable in excess of half an inch or so

---

* Don't mess with air dielectric unless you enjoy the challenge of keeping your feed lines pressurized with nitrogen. Air dielectric cable at 802.11b power levels is like the proverbial elephant gun to kill the mosquito.

in thickness is difficult to work with and can be hard to find connectors for. Whenever possible, order the specific length you need, with the proper connectors preinstalled, rather than trying to cut and crimp it yourself. A commercial outlet will usually have the tools and experience needed to make a well-built cable. The best cable in the world won't help you if your connector isn't properly installed.

Table 6-1. Attenuation, size, and approximate cost of microwave coax

Cable type	Diameter	Loss in dB/100′ at 2500MHz	Approximate price per foot
LMR-200	0.195″	16.9	$0.37
LMR-400	0.405″	6.8	$0.64
LMR-600	0.509″	4.4	$1.30
LMR-900	0.870″	3.0	$3.70
LMR-1200	1.200″	2.3	$5.50
Belden 9913	0.405″	8.2	$0.97
LDF1-50	0.250″	6.1	$1.66
LDF4-50A	0.500″	3.9	$3.91
LDF5-50A	0.875″	2.3	$2.27
LDF6-50	1.250″	1.7	$10.94
LDF7-50A	1.625″	1.4	$15.76

To sum up: use the best quality cable you can afford at the shortest length possible. A couple of dB here and there really adds up. If you want to put an antenna on the roof, look into weatherproof enclosures for your router and mount it as close to the antenna as possible. Then run your Ethernet cable as long as you need (up to 100 meters!).

Connectors

You have the radio, an antenna, and a length of cable. How do you connect them together? You need to use connectors that work well in the 2.4GHz range, fit the kind of cabling you're using, and mate with each other. Practically all common connectors have two halves, a male and a female (or pin and socket). A few of the more exotic types (like the APC-7) are sexless, so any connector will match up with any other. Here are the most common connectors you are likely to encounter in the microwave bestiary.

The Bayonet Navy Connector (BNC) is a small, cheap connector using a quick-connect half turn (the same connector found on 10base2 Ethernet). The BNC (shown in Figure 6-12) isn't well suited for 2.4GHz use, but it is mentioned here because, with the death of 10base2, the connectors are frequently sold for pennies per pound. Don't be tempted.

Figure 6-12. BNC: Bayonet Navy Connector (or Bayonet Neill Concelman, depending on who you ask)

The TNC (see Figure 6-13) is a threaded version of the BNC. The fine threads help eliminate leakage at microwave frequencies. TNCs work well all the way through 12GHz and are often used with smaller (and higher loss) cable.

Figure 6-13. TNC (threaded BNC)

An N ("Navy" or "Neill") connector is a larger, threaded connector found on many commercial 2.4GHz antennas (see Figure 6-14). It is much larger than the TNC. It works very well on thicker cable (like LMR-400) and operates well up to 10GHz. The N is probably the most commonly encountered connector when dealing with 802.11b-compatible gear.

Figure 6-14. N connector

The so-called UHF connector looks like a coarse-thread version of the N (see Figure 6-15). It's not usable for 2.4GHz, but it is frequently confused with the N. According to the ARRL Microwave manual, it's a PL-259 (which mates with the SO-239 socket). It's not designed to work at microwave frequencies. You should avoid it.

Figure 6-15. The so-called "UHF" connector

The SMA connector (Figure 6-16) is a very popular, small, threaded connector that works great through 18GHz. Their small size precludes using them with large, low-loss cable.

The SMB (Figure 6-17) is a quick-connect version of the SMC.

The SMC (see Figure 6-18) is a very small version of the SMA. It's good through 10GHz, but it accepts only *very* small (high-loss) cables. If only radio manufacturers had standardized on this as the external antenna connector of choice, there would be no call for custom pigtails.

Figure 6-16. SMA: Sub-Miniature connector, variation A

Figure 6-17. SMB: Sub-Miniature connector, variation B

The APC-7 (Figure 6-19) is a 7mm sexless connector, usable through 18GHz. It is a high-grade connector manufactured by Amphenol, and it is expensive, fairly rare, and very low loss.

Remember that each connector in the system introduces some loss. Avoid adapters and unnecessary connectors whenever possible. Also, commercially built cables tend to be of higher quality than cables you terminate yourself (unless you're really good and have the right tools). Whenever possible, try to buy a pre-made cable with the proper connectors already attached, at the shortest length you can stand. 802.11b gear doesn't put out

Figure 6-18. SMC: Sub-Miniature connector, variation C

Figure 6-19. APC-7: Amphenol Precision Connector

much power, and every little bit helps extend your range and reliability. It's very easy to make a bad cable, and bad cables can cause no end of trouble.

When matching cables to your equipment, you may encounter connectors of reverse gender (male and female swapped, with same threads), reverse threading (lefthand instead of righthand thread), or even reverse gender reverse threading (both). Make sure you know what you're getting before you order parts online!

On outdoor installations, proper lightning protection is vital. Gas tube lightning arrestors (see Figure 6-20) can provide a high degree of protection (both for your equipment and against fire) from lightning strikes to your antenna.

They cost anywhere from $30–100, and they can provide multistrike protection when properly installed. Be sure to read up on proper installation, use good quality grounding line, and, when in doubt, call in a professional. Most arrestors I've seen have female N connectors on either end, so be sure to factor that in when considering your hardware installation.

Figure 6-20. A gas tube lightning arrestor

Calculating Range

How far will your signal go? That's a very good question. It depends on all sorts of factors, including the power output and sensitivity of your card, the quality of your cable, connectors, and antenna, intervening clutter and noise, and even weather patterns (on long distance links). While it's impossible to take all of these variables precisely into account, you can make a good estimate before buying any hardware. Here's a simple way to build an estimate (frequently referred to as your *link budget*).

First, figure out how much loss the signal will incur in the space between the two sites. This is called the *path loss*. One common formula for estimating path loss at 2.4GHz is:

$$L = 20 \log(d) + 20 \log(f) + 36.6$$

where L is the loss in dB, d is the distance in miles, and f is the frequency in megahertz.

Suppose you wanted to set up a five-mile link between two points, using channel 6 (2.437 GHz):

$$L = 20 \log(5) + 20 \log(2437) + 36.6$$
$$L = (20 \times 0.69) + (20 \times 3.38) + 36.6$$
$$L = 13.8 + 67.6 + 36.6$$
$$L = 118$$

At five miles, with no obstacles in between, you will lose 118 dB of signal between the two points. Our link must tolerate that much loss (plus a bit extra to account for weather and miscellaneous interference) or it will be unreliable.

Next, add up all of your gains (radios + antennas + amplifiers) and subtract your losses (cable length, connectors, lightning arrestors, and miscellaneous other losses). Let's assume you are using Orinoco Silver cards (15dBm), no amplifiers, with a 12dBi sector on one side, and a 15dBi yagi on the other. We'll assume you're using one meter of LMR-400 and a lightning arrestor on each side, allowing 0.25dB loss for each connector, and 1dB for each pigtail. Since all of the units are in dB, we can use simple addition and subtraction:

radio - pigtail - arrestor - connector - cable - connector + antenna
Site A: 15 - 1 - 1.25 - 0.25 - 0.22 - 0.25 + 12 = 24.03
Site B: 15 - 1 - 1.25 - 0.25 - 0.22 - 0.25 + 15 = 27.03
A + B = 51.06 total gain

Now, subtract the path loss from that total:

51.06 - 118 = −66.94

This is the perceived signal level at each end of the link: -66.94dBm. But is it enough for communications?

Looking up the receiver sensitivity specs for the Orinoco Silver card (you have to look for it, but it is buried in the manual), we find the results shown in Table 6-2.

Table 6-2. Receiver sensitivity matrix for Orinoco Silver cards

11Mbps	5.5Mbps	2Mbps	1Mbps
-82 dBm	-87 dBm	-91 dBm	-94 dBm

Because we are generating a signal of −66.94dBm, we have a "fudge factor" of 15.06dB (82 - 66.94 = 15.06). Theoretically, this will usually work at 11Mbps (in good weather) and should have no problem syncing at 5.5Mbps. The radios should automatically sense when the link becomes unreliable and resync at the fastest possible speed.

Typically, a margin of error of 20dB or so is safe enough to account for normal intervening weather patterns. Using more powerful radios (such as the Cisco 350, at 20dBm) or higher gain antennas would help shore up this connection to 11Mbps. Using higher gain cards (such as the Cisco or Teletronics cards) in conjunction with high gain dishes make it possible to extend your range well beyond 25 miles.

Online tools like Green Bay Professional Packet Radio's Wireless Network Link Analysis can give you a good ballpark estimate on what it will take to make your link possible; you just fill in a couple of blanks on a web form. Check out their excellent resources at *http://www.gbonline.com/~multiplx/wireless/page09.html*.

Power Amps and the Law

Frequently, when people think of extending range, they immediately think of using amplifiers (I suppose it's only natural; you have an amplifier for your home stereo, why not an amplifier for your network?). Good amplifiers that work in the microwave range have several nontrivial technical obstacles to overcome:

- Amplifiers blindly amplify everything that they're tuned to, both signal and noise. A greater signal won't help you if the noise in the band is increased as well, because the signal will just get lost (like shouting to your friends at a concert).

- 802.11b radio communications are half duplex; they send or receive, but never both at the same time. An amplifier attached to the antenna line will have to detect automatically when the radio is sending and quickly switch the amp on. When it's finished, it has to quickly cut it off again. Any latency in this switching could actually impair communications or, worse, damage the radio card.

- Amplifiers can help a bit on receive by adding some pre-emphasis, but they are really meant for transmitting. This means that if you only have an amp on one end of a link, the other end may be able to hear you, but you may not hear them. To make amps effective, you'll need them on both ends of the link.

- All amplifiers require power to operate. This means adding a DC injector to your antenna feed line or using an external adapter. This further drives up the cost of your node and makes yet another device that you have to provide power for.

As a result, amplifiers that work well with 802.11b gear are expensive ($400+) and difficult to come by. But do you really need them? Using standard gear and high gain antennas, you can extend a point-to-point link to 25+ miles without amplifiers. Your money is probably better spent on high-quality directional antennas and cabling, and possibly even adding another node for further saturation.

As far as U.S. federal law is concerned, you'll have to read the Part 15 (see the Appendix) and draw your own conclusions. Hire a lawyer if you're really paranoid. Tim Pozar (of the BAWUG) has made some interesting observations about the Part 15 rules regarding 2.4GHz emissions; check out his commentary online at *http://www.lns.com/papers/FCCPart15_and_the_ISM_2.4G_Band.index*.

In short, the amount of power you can legally run (and the gain of your antenna) is limited, depending on how you use it. Fixed point-to-point links are allotted the most power, while omnidirectional point-to-multipoint configurations are the most restricted. Unless you use amplifiers, you probably aren't likely to run into the FCC limits, because standard client cards don't put out nearly enough power. But don't just take my word for it, because I am not a lawyer (besides, the person responsible for making sure that your rig is legal is you, the operator!)

I do believe that the intent behind the rules is to limit interference in the band, which is something we should all fight to make happen. Noise is everyone's enemy. To that end, try to use the least amount of power necessary to keep your link going, and use the most directional antennas that will work for your application. Be a good neighbor, and you may find that you enjoy your neighborhood more.

CHAPTER 7
Other Applications

Thanks to the efforts of countless engineers, we have an open 802.11b standard. Now that hardware that adheres to this standard is in the hands of non-engineers, all sorts of interesting applications have been implemented. Thousands around the globe are pushing the capabilities of these inexpensive radios well beyond their intended limits. Standard client PCMCIA cards have been used to create point-to-point backbone links several miles apart. Not content with tiny, private networks, people are using inexpensive access points to create public networks that can support hundreds of simultaneous users. Even the popularized security shortcomings of 802.11b are being overcome by some careful planning and the proper application of open source software. Whether the IEEE committee intended it to be so or not, 802.11b has stumbled on the magic formula that makes the ultimate platform for hardware hackery: low cost, ease of use, ease of modification, and ubiquity.

In this chapter, we'll take a look at some wireless applications that demonstrate the enormous flexibility of wireless (and some that are just really cool!). Be warned that some of the examples in this chapter will certainly void warrantees and may damage your equipment if you're not careful. If you are ever unsure about how to proceed, ask around. Chances are, someone else has done what you're thinking of doing and can at least lend you their shared experience. The various wireless group mailing lists are a great resource for ideas and working out implementation details.

Point-to-Point Links

From a radio perspective, point-to-point links are very straightforward to set up. You should always follow more or less the same steps when evaluating the possibility of a link:

- Establish that you have line of sight from end to end.

- Measure the distance between the points and calculate the path loss.
- Add the capabilities of your equipment to determine your link budget.
- Go out and hook up your gear.

If you intend to make a long-distance point-to-point link, first find out the latitude, longitude, and altitude of each end point. You can find this by physically going to each site and marking the coordinates with a GPS, or you can estimate using topographical maps or software (see Chapter 6 for some examples of how to do this). With the coordinates and altitude of both sites, you can calculate a bearing and tilt angle, so you know roughly where to point the antennas on each end. A decent GPS can help here by giving you a bearing to and from each point. You should also check out the online wireless design CGIs at *http://www.gbonline.com/~multiplx/wireless/page09.html* for help with many of the calculations you'll need to perform.

Obviously, if you can see the other point through binoculars or a telescope, this is a good first step. Ideally, there should be very little on the ground between the two points. The closer the path is to an actual valley, the better. Take a look at Chapter 6 for details about how to calculate the path loss and link budget for your link. I've mentioned it before, but here it is again: keep your antenna cable as short as possible! On a long-distance point-to-point link, every few decibels count.

Now that you're ready to hook up your gear, the question remains: what gear do you want to use? That depends on your budget and how you plan to use the link. As we saw in Chapter 5, it is very simple to set up a Linux gateway in IBSS mode. This is probably the cheapest way to go for each end, but it presents some routing issues (most wireless cards disable Ethernet bridging, so you'll need to use masquerading to get packets to flow across the wireless link). If you already have a hardware access point, you can use it for one end of the link and a client card for the other, with the same configuration (i.e., masquerading on the client side). A recently released, low-cost hardware alternative is the Linksys WAP-11 access point. Linksys has released a firmware upgrade that allows this AP to communicate with others (of the same model) over the air, either in point-to-point or point-to-multipoint mode. You can download Version 1.4f.5 from their web site at *http://www.linksys.com*. These access points sell for around $200 and include reverse gender TNC external antenna connectors, so this can be a very inexpensive choice for setting up a point-to-point link.

The farther apart your points are, the harder it will be to aim your antennas. At distances up to five miles or so, this is rarely a problem (as long as you have enough total gain to overcome the path loss). At greater distances, getting the antennas pointed directly at each other can be quite tricky. Here are a few techniques that might help you get your dishes pointed where they need to be:

- Use cell phones or radios to maintain communications between the two points while you're aiming the antennas. It helps to have at least two people at each end (one to manipulate the antenna, and another to coordinate with the other end).

- Set up all your network settings ahead of time, so there aren't any variables once you get to the remote site. Check all gear, ping each box, and even transfer a file or two to be sure that your equipment works at close range. You don't want to question it later if you have problems getting the link going.

- Use a tool like the Lucent Link Test meter (which ships with the Windows driver for the Orinoco card) to show the signal strength and noise readings in real time. This kind of tool is your best friend, short of an actual spectrum analyzer.

- Work on one end of the link at a time, slowly changing one variable at a time until you see the maximum signal strength and lowest noise.

- If you have one handy (and if your link budget permits it), first try an omni or sector antenna on one end of the link. Once you find the other end of the link, replace it with your dish or yagi, and tune it in.

- Sweep slowly, and don't be afraid to go beyond the best perceived signal. Most antennas have smaller side lobes that appear as a false positive. Keep moving until you find the main lobe. It should stand out significantly from the others, once you find it.

- Do *not* touch the actual antenna when taking a reading. This is particularly easy to overlook when using tube yagis, like the Pringles can (see the next section). Resting your hand on the antenna tube will interfere with the radiation pattern and drain your signal very quickly. Take your readings with all hands clear of the equipment.

- Don't forget to compare horizontal and vertical polarization. Try the antennas in both positions, and use the one that shows the lowest noise (see the section "Redundant Links" later in this chapter).

- Once your link is in place, consider using WEP to discourage others from attempting to connect to it. If you want to provide wireless access at either endpoint, set up another gateway, preferably with caching services (such as caching DNS and a transparent web proxy, like Squid). This helps reduce the amount of traffic that goes over the long link, cuts down on network collisions, and generally makes more efficient use of the link.

It can take all day to properly align antennas at a great distance, but it can also be a fun time with the right group of people. Just take your time, think about what you're doing, and be sure to leave time at the end of the day to celebrate!

The Pringles Can

At the Portland Summit last June, Andrew Clapp (*http://www.netscum.com/~clap/*) presented a novel yagi antenna design. It used a bolt, metal tubing, washers, and PVC tubing to make an inexpensive "shotgun" yagi, either 18" or 36" long. While his antenna shows between 12 and 15dBi gain (which is impressive for such a simple design), it's also quite large. When we returned from Portland, some members of our local group and I realized that, if we were careful, we could fit a full wavelength inside a Pringles can, as shown in Figure 7-1. This would show a reduced total gain, but it would also make the entire antenna much more compact.

Figure 7-1. The complete antenna—it's just a can!

Parts List

Here are the items you'll need to make a Pringles can antenna:

Part	Approximate cost
All-thread, 5 5/8" long, 1/8" OD	$1.00
two nylon lock nuts	$0.10
five 1" washers, 1/8" ID	$0.10

Part	Approximate cost
6" aluminum tubing, 1/4" ID	$0.75
A connector to match your radio pigtail (we used a female N connector)	$3.00
1 1/2" piece of 12-gauge solid copper wire (we used ground wire from house electrical wiring)	negligible
A tall Pringles can (any flavor, Ridges are optional)	$1.50
Scrap plastic disc, 3" across (like another Pringles can lid)	negligible
TOTAL	$6.45

Of course, buying in bulk helps a lot. You probably won't be able to find a 6-inch piece of all-thread; buy the standard size (usually one or two feet) and a 10-pack of washers and nuts while you're at it. Then you'll have more than enough parts to make two, all for about $10.

Required Tools

You'll need the following tools to make your antenna:

- Ruler
- Scissors
- Pipe cutter (or hacksaw or Dremel tool, in a pinch)
- Heavy-duty cutters (or Dremel again, to cut the all-thread)
- Something sharp to pierce the plastic (like an awl or a drill bit)
- Hot glue gun (unless you have a screw-down type connector)
- Soldering iron

Construction time should be about an hour.

Front Collector Construction

Mark and cut four pieces of tubing, about 1.2 inches (1 15/64 inches). Where did I get this number? First. figure out the wavelength at the bottom of the frequency range we're using (2.412 GHz, or channel 1). This will be the longest that the pipe should be:

$$W = 3.0 \times 10^8 \times (1 / 2.412) \times 10^{-9}$$
$$W = (3.0 / 2.412) \times 10^{-1}$$
$$W = 0.124 \text{ meters}$$
$$W = 4.88 \text{ inches}$$

We'll be cutting the pipe to quarter wavelength, so:

$$1/4 \ W = 4.88 / 4$$
$$1/4 \ W = 1.22 \text{ inches}$$

Now figure out what the shortest length we'll ever use is (2.462GHz, or channel 11 in the United States):

$$W = 3.0 \times 10^8 \times (1 / 2.462) \times 10^{-9}$$
$$W = (3.0 / 2.462) \times 10^{-1}$$
$$W = 0.122 \text{ meters}$$
$$W = 4.80 \text{ inches}$$
$$1/4\ W = 1.20 \text{ inches}$$

Practically speaking, what's the difference between the shortest pipe and the longest pipe length? About 0.02 inches, or less than 1/32 inch. That's probably about the size of the pipe cutter blade you're using. So, just shoot for 1.2 inches, and you'll get it close enough.

Cut the all-thread to exactly 5 5/8 inches. The washers we used are about 1/16 inch thick, so that should leave just enough room for the pipe, washers, and nuts.

Pierce a hole in the center of the Pringles can lid big enough for the all-thread to pass through. Now is probably a good time to start eating Pringles (we found it better for all concerned to just toss the things; the salt and vinegar–flavor chips are almost caustic after the first fifteen or so).

Cut a 3-inch plastic disc just big enough to fit snugly inside the can. We found that another Pringles lid, with the outer ridge trimmed off, works just fine. Poke a hole in the center of it, and slip it over one of the lengths of pipe.

Now, assemble the pipe. You might have to use a file or Dremel tool to shave the tips of the thread if you have trouble getting the nuts on. The pipe is a sandwich that goes on the all-thread as shown in Figure 7-2.

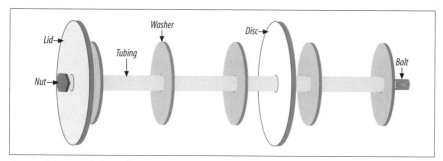

Figure 7-2. Nut, lid, washer, pipe, washer, pipe, washer, pipe-with-plastic, washer, pipe, washer, nut

Tighten down the nuts to be snug, but don't overtighten (I bent the tubing on our first try; aluminum bends *very* easily). Just get it snug. Congratulations, you now have the front collector, just like the one shown in Figure 7-2.

Preparing the Can

By now you should have eaten (or tossed) the actual chips. Wipe out the can, and measure 3 3/8 inches up from the bottom of the can. Cut a hole just big enough for the connector to pass through. We found through trial and error that this seems to be the "sweet spot" of the can. On our Pringles Salt & Vinegar can, the N connector sat directly between "Sodium" and "Protein."

Element Construction

Straighten the heavy copper wire and solder it to the connector. When inside the can, the wire should be just below the midpoint of the can (ours turned out to be about 1 1/16 inches). You lose a few dB by going longer, so cut it just shy of the middle of the can.

We were in a hurry, so we used hot glue to hold the connector in place on our first antenna. If you have a connector that uses a nut and washer, and you're really careful about cutting the hole, these work very well (and aren't nearly as messy as hot glue). Just remember that you're screwing into cardboard when you connect your pigtail. It's very easy to forget and accidentally tear the wall of the can.

Now, insert the collector assembly into the can and close the lid. The inside end of the pipe should *not* touch the copper element; it should be just forward of it. If it touches, your all-thread is probably too long. Figure 7-3 shows a completed antenna.

How can one estimate gain without access to high-end radio analysis gear? Using the Link Test software that comes with the Orinoco Silver cards, you can see the signal and noise readings (in dB) of a received signal and your test partner's reception of your signal. As I happen to live 0.6 mile (with clean line of sight) from O'Reilly headquarters, we had a fairly controlled testbed to experiment with. We shot at the omni on the roof and used the access point at O'Reilly as our link test partner.

To estimate antenna performance, we started by connecting commercial antennas of known gain and taking readings. Then we connected our test antennas and compared the results. We had the following at our disposal:

- Two 10dBi, 180-degree sector panel antennas
- One 11dBi, 120-degree sector panel antenna
- One 24dBi parabolic dish
- A couple of Pringles cans and some hardware

Figure 7-3. The completed antenna

Here were the average received signal and noise readings from each, in approximately the same physical position:

Antenna	Signal	Noise
10dBi A	-83db	-92db
10dBi B	-83db	-92db
11dBi	-82db	-95db
24dBi	-67db	-102db
Pringles can	-81db	-98db

The test partner (AP side) signal results were virtually the same. Interestingly, even at only 0.6 mile, we saw some thermal fade effect; as the evening turned into night, we saw about 3dB gain across the board. (It had been a particularly hot day, almost 100 degrees. I don't know what the relative humidity was, but it felt fairly dry.)

Yagis and dishes are much more directional than sectors and omnis. This bore out in the numbers, as the perceived noise level was consistently lower with the more directional antennas. This can help a lot on long distance shots, because not only will your perceived signal be greater, the competing noise will seem to be less. More directional antennas also help keep noise down for your neighbors trying to share the spectrum as well. Be a good neighbor and use the most directional antennas that will work for your application (yes, noise is everybody's problem).

The Pringles can seemed to have large side lobes that extend about 45 degrees from the center of the can. Don't point the can directly at where you're trying to go; aim slightly to the left or the right. We also found that elevating the antenna helped a bit as well. When aiming the antenna, hold it behind the connector, and *slowly* sweep from left to right, with the Link Test program running. When you get the maximum signal, slowly raise the end of the can to see if it makes a difference. Go slowly, changing only one variable at a time.

Remember that the can is polarized, so match the phase of the antenna you're talking to. For example, if shooting at an omni, be sure the element is on the bottom or the top of the can, or you won't be able to see it! See the earlier discussion on antenna polarization for more information on how you can use this effect to your advantage.

We were fortunate enough to have a member of our community group bring a return loss meter to one of our meetings, and we were able to get some actual measurements of how much signal was returning to the radio. The results weren't as good as I had hoped, but they showed that the antenna was usable, particularly at lower frequencies. Most likely, failing to take into account the thickness of the washers has made the entire front element a little too long. There isn't nearly enough power leaving the radio to cause damage due to high return loss, but it does point out that the antenna isn't as well tuned as it could be.

We haven't looked into weatherproof housing for the can; sinking the whole thing into some 3-inch PVC should do the trick. Over a clear line of sight, with short antenna cable runs, a 12dB to 12dB can-to-can shot should be able to carry an 11Mbps link well over ten miles. You can check out our progress with the can online at *http://nocat.net*.

Redundant Links

All antennas show a characteristic known as polarity, which refers to the direction that the electrical field moves in as it leaves the antenna. Simultaneously, magnetic waves leave the antenna at a 90-degree angle to the electrical waves. Most common antennas show a linear polarity (i.e., vertical or horizontal). Some antennas, like a wound helical antenna,* actually demonstrate circular polarity, where the waves move outward in a spiral, always perpendicular to each other.

In order for one antenna to be able to receive the signals of another, the polarity must match. Omnidirectionals (and most sectors) have vertical polarity. Dishes and yagis can be mounted vertically, horizontally, or somewhere in between. The Pringles can is just a yagi, and its polarity is determined by the position of the antenna connector. A circularly polarized antenna (like the helical) has its polarity determined by the direction of the outer winding: either clockwise or counterclockwise!

You can use polarity to your advantage to try to eliminate some noise on a long-distance link. First try each end in vertical polarization and measure the perceived noise. Then rotate each end 90 degrees and measure the noise again. Use the position that shows the least amount of noise, and you should have a more stable link.

Since an antenna can receive signals only from antennas whose polarity matches its own, you can also use this property to make more efficient redundant links. For example, suppose you wanted to use two radios at either end of a link to provide 22Mbps total bandwidth to a remote location. Usually, you would need to use two channels separated by 25MHz (i.e. , 1 and 6, or 2 and 7, or 3 and 8). If you use one antenna with vertical polarization and another with horizontal polarization and separate the antennas by a few feet, you could use the same channel for all of your traffic. This means less noise in the band for yourself and your neighbors (and it theoretically gives you up to 6 possible simultaneous links, where normally only 3 were possible).

As far as IP goes, you can either route the traffic independently or use the channel bonding features of the Linux 2.4 kernel to weld all of your connections into one big pipe. This mode of operations is new, experimental, and left as an exercise for the reader (hey, if you're anything like me, you could stand more exercise in your life).

Repeaters

Unfortunately, long distance line of sight isn't always possible. Sometimes, you will encounter an obstacle that you simply can't go over (or through). Or you might need to stretch a link to go farther than your available radios and antennas permit. Maybe you are just on the edge of range of a good AP

---

* See *http://users.bigpond.net.au/jhecker/* for details and plans for this interesting design!

but need to provide access to a room full of people (and they don't all have high-gain antennas). A repeater may help in your application.

A radio repeater is a piece of equipment with two complete radios in it. Any traffic heard on the first radio is repeated to the second, and vice versa. If directional antennas are used, a weak signal reaching one of the transmitters is then rebroadcast over the other channel, as if it had originated from that point. Figure 7-4 shows the use of this technique to extend range or get around obstacles.

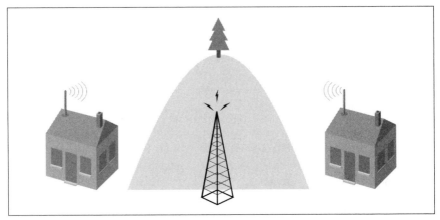

Figure 7-4. A repeater does just that: repeat everything it hears to someone else down the line

While a classic radio repeater might work fine with 802.11b, I unfortunately don't have access to radio gear capable of broadcasting a 25MHz wide signal at 2.4GHz. But I do have the next best thing: a couple of 802.11b PCMCIA cards.

The following sections describe two repeater-like configurations that I've used successfully.

Two Cards in One PC

If you have a PC with two PCMCIA slots, you can configure Linux to use both interfaces, and pass packets between them. Insert two wireless cards, and you have the hardware needed for a repeater application. While many client cards specifically disable Ethernet bridging, you can still use masquerading between the interfaces to bring two networks together.

One intriguing portable device that works well as a repeater is the Fujitsu Stylistic 1000. It is an old 486/100 tablet PC that comes with a monochrome LCD screen, stylus, 200MB PCMCIA hard drive, no keyboard, all of the usual PC ports, a lithium ion battery, and two extra PCMCIA slots. You can pick them up through used parts suppliers for around $100. (Thanks to the BAWUG crew for finding these nifty little devices!)

Take a look at Chapter 5 for details on how to get Linux installed and configured for masquerading. Once the software is configured, the only remaining issue is this: how do you squeeze one card on top of the other? Most wireless cards have a slight protruding bulge to make room for their internal antenna and won't fit in a stacked PCMCIA bay.

There are a couple of ways around this problem. Obviously, if you're using a card like the Cisco LMC35x for the bottom card, there is no bulge and therefore no problem. If you're using a card like the D-Link DWL-650,* the bulge is small enough that you can just squeeze two cards in at the same time. If you're using an Orinoco card on the bottom, your only recourse is to pop the plastic cover off and remove the two silver internal antenna tabs. This makes the card more or less useless without an external antenna, but it can be worth it if you're pressed for time (or cash) and have a card that you're willing to dedicate to long distance work. Remember to connect an external antenna to both radios when using two in one machine, or else the transmitters will be operating right next to each other, and cause a tremendous amount of interference.

This technique, shown in Figure 7-5, is very inexpensive, but it has the serious drawback that the two networks aren't actually bridged but are connected through a NAT box. While this may suit your purposes, it won't help much if both networks need to contact each other directly. If you need bridging between networks, look into higher-end equipment, such as the Cisco Ethernet Bridge or Orinoco AP-1000. Alternatively, you might try the method described in the following section.

Two APs Back-to-Back

Many access points are capable of bridging the wireless network directly to the wire. What happens if you connect two APs in bridging mode back-to-back over a crossover CAT5 cable? Naturally, you have a bridging repeater.

I have only tried this with two Apple AirPorts, shown in Figure 7-6, but theoretically any AP capable of bridge mode should work fine. In this configuration, anyone within range of access point A will have their traffic repeated verbatim to access point B, and vice versa. As the Apple AirPorts actually use Orinoco Silver radio cards, the necessary external antenna connectors

---

* See *http://kevlar.burdell.org/~will/antenna/* for one quick way to add an external antenna to the DWL-650.

Figure 7-5. Two Orinoco cards in one

are already present inside the UFO. In fact, by removing the outer shell, it is possible to mount both AirPorts in a single, small, weatherproof box, with each connected to its own directional antenna. Each AirPort can even be configured with its own channel and security settings, if necessary. Performance won't be as optimal as with a straight shot (because you have doubled your chances of a data collision), but it can make a connection possible where one might otherwise not be.

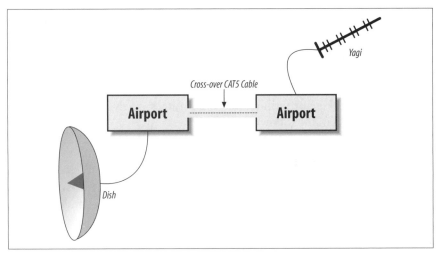

Figure 7-6. Two Apple AirPorts in bridge mode, connected with a crossover cable, can act as an 802.11b repeater

Security Concerns

When using an open wireless network, all traffic between your laptop and the access point is sent in the clear to anyone in range. When using WEP, anyone who shares the same WEP key can listen in on your traffic as if it were an open network. How can you protect your data from prying eyes while using wireless? The best possible protection is provided by end-to-end encryption. This is provided by tools such as SSL, PPTP, and SSH. For example, browsing to an SSL-enabled web page will keep your conversation private, leaving any would-be eavesdroppers with data that looks much like line noise. The encryption and identification facilities provided by the 128-bit SSL implementation are widely regarded as good enough for use over untrusted networks, like wireless.

SSL may be fine for web pages (and some mail clients), but what about protecting other traffic? This section describes one method for securing your email using OpenSSH.* For a more thorough exploration of the possibilities of SSH, I highly recommend *SSH: The Secure Shell*, also published by O'Reilly.

OpenSSH is being developed for BSD, but thanks to the great work by their porting team, it compiles under many Unix-like operating systems (including Linux, Solaris, HP/UX, MacOS X, and many others). You can even use it in Windows, using the Cygwin package. Check out *http://www.cygwin.com* and download it now, if you haven't already. It almost makes Windows fun to use!

Download OpenSSH and build it. You'll also need a copy of the OpenSSL libraries to compile OpenSSH. You can get OpenSSL from *http://www. openssl.org*. Once you've installed OpenSSH, you can use it to tunnel POP traffic from your local laptop to your mail server (called "mailhost"). We'll assume you have a shell account on the mail server for this example, although any machine on your internal network that accepts SSH connections should suffice.

Establish the Connection

Under OpenSSH:

```
laptop# ssh -L 110:mailhost:110 -l user -N mailhost
```

(Naturally, substitute user with your username and mailhost with your mail server's hostname or IP address.) Note that you will have to be root on your laptop for this example, since you'll be binding to a privileged port (110, the POP port). You should also disable any locally running POP daemon (look in */etc/inetd.conf*), or it will get in the way.

---

* OpenSSH is a free, open source implementation of the SSH protocol. You can get it online at *http: //www.openssh.com*.

Assuming you have your RSA or DSA keys set up, you can even run this in the background (just tack on an &). This sets up the tunnel, and starts forwarding your local ports to the remote end through it. The -N switch tells SSH to not bother running an actual command on the remote end and to just do the forwarding.

Configure Your Mail Software

You now need to tell your mail software to connect to your tunnel rather than connecting to your mail server directly. This is different in each application, but the idea is always the same: you want your email client to connect to *localhost* instead of *mailhost*.

Here's how to set it up under Netscape Communicator; other clients may have different menu choices, but the principle is the same:

- Go to Edit → Preferences.
- Expand the Mail & Newsgroups tree, and select Mail Servers.
- Remove your existing incoming mail server, and add a new one.
- Under General, type localhost as the Server Name. Select POP3 as the Server Type.
- Hit OK, make sure your tunnel is established, and retrieve your mail.

Naturally, it doesn't have to end with POP. You can also forward SMTP for outgoing mail (port 25). Simply specify multiple -L entries, like this:

```
laptop# ssh -L 110:mailhost:110 -L 25:mailhost:25 -l user -N mailhost
```

Now just set your outgoing mail server to *localhost,* and all of your incoming and outgoing email will be protected from prying eyes (er, ears) on your wireless network.

Captive "Catch and Release" Portal

While some node owners are perfectly happy opening their networks to whoever happens to be in range, most of us hesitate at the thought of paying for our neighbors to use our bandwidth. After all, apart from using up resources that we're paying for, anonymous users could potentially abuse other networks and have their shenanigans traced back to our network! If we want to provide responsible wireless access, we need a way to securely identify users when they connect and then allocate only the resources that the node owner is willing to contribute. After the Portland Summit, it was obvious that one key component that was missing from the community network idea was a freely available *captive portal* implementation.

The idea behind a captive portal is fairly straightforward. Rather than relying on the built-in security features of 802.11b to control who can associate with an AP, we configure the access point with no WEP and as an open network. The AP is also in bridged mode and connected via a crossover cable to an Ethernet card on a Linux router. It is then up to the router to issue DHCP leases, throttle bandwidth, and permit access to other networks. When a user attempts to browse to any web page, they are redirected to a page that presents the user with a login prompt and information about the node they are connected to. If the wireless gateway has a method of contacting a central authority to determine the identity of the connected wireless user, then it can relax its firewall rules appropriately, allowing the privileges due that user (for example, more bandwidth or access to other machines and ports).

The *NoCatAuth* project implements such a third-party authentication system (or Auth system, for short). Written in Perl and C, it takes care of presenting the user with a login prompt, contacts a MySQL database to look up user credentials, securely notifies the wireless gateway of the user's status, and authorizes further access. On the gateway side, the software manages local connections, sets bandwidth throttling and firewall rules, and times out old logins after a user specified time limit. The software is released under the GPL.

We are designing the system so that trust is ultimately preserved; the gateways and end users need only trust the Auth system, which is secured with a registered SSL certificate. Passwords are never given to the wireless gateway (thus protecting the users from "bad guy" node owners), and gateway rules are modified only by a cryptographically signed message from the Auth system (protecting the gateway from users or upstream sites trying to spoof the Auth system).

We provide for three possible classes of wireless user:

- Public Class
- Co-op Class
- Owner Class

A *Public Class* user would be someone who knows nothing about the local wireless group and is simply looking for access to the Internet. This class is granted very little bandwidth, and users are restricted in what services they can access by the use of firewall rules. The Public Class of user is given the opportunity to learn more about who is providing the wireless service and how they can get in touch with the local group (and ultimately get more access). They do not have personal logins but must still authenticate by manually skipping the login process (hence the term *catch and release*).

The *Co-op Class* consists of users with prearranged login information. The rules for membership should be determined by the local community groups and are configured in the central Auth system database. This class is typically granted much greater bandwidth and access to ports, as users can now be held accountable for their own actions.

The *Owner Class* is much the same as the Co-op Class, but it is reserved for the owner of a given node and anyone else to whom they want to grant access. The Owner Class preempts traffic from all other classes and has free use of all network resources.

The typical connection process starts when a roaming user associates with the AP and is immediately issued a DHCP lease, as shown in Figure 7-7. All access beyond contacting the Auth service is denied by default. When the user tries to browse the Web, he is immediately redirected to the gateway service, which then redirects him to the Auth system's SSL login page (after appending a random token and some other information to the URL line).

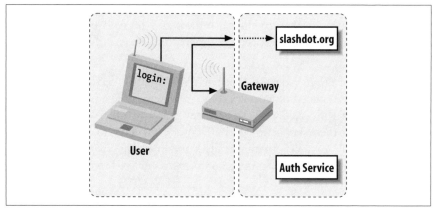

Figure 7-7. User is immediately issued a lease, and their first web connection is redirected to the wireless gateway's service

The user is then presented with three choices: login with his prearranged login information, click on a link to find out more about membership, or click the *Skip Login* button.

Once the user has either logged in correctly or skipped the process, the Auth system then creates an outcome message, signs it with PGP, and sends it back to the wireless gateway (see Figure 7-8). The gateway has a copy of the Auth service's public PGP key and can verify the authenticity of the message. Part of the data included in the response is the random token that the gateway originally issued to the client, making it very difficult to fake out the gateway with a "replay attack." The digital signature prevents the possibility of other machines posing as the Auth service and sending bogus messages to the wireless gateway.

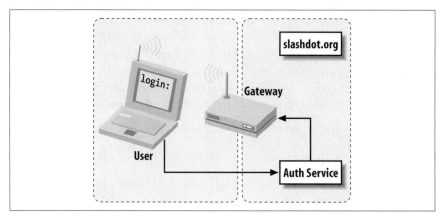

Figure 7-8. After login, the Auth system connects back to the wireless gateway and notifies it of the outcome; the gateway can then decide whether or not to grant further access

Now, if all has gone well for the user, the wireless gateway modifies its firewall rules to grant further access and redirects the user back to the site he were originally trying to browse (as shown in Figure 7-9).

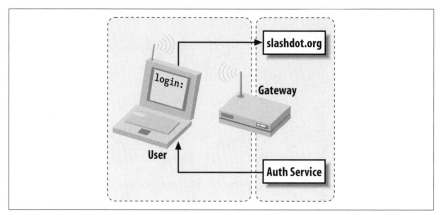

Figure 7-9. The user can now continue along his merry way

In order to keep the connection open, a small window is opened on the client side (via JavaScript) that refreshes the login page every few minutes. Once the user moves out of range or quits his browser, the connection is reset and requires another manual login.

The requirements on the gateway side are minimal (the system was designed to run under Linux 2.4.5 on a 486 with 16MB RAM). The Auth service is designed to be administered by a community group that maintains its user database in whatever way they see fit. For example, running a node is one obvious way to become a co-op member. But that isn't always the best way to spend resources; people who contribute hardware, programming skill, bandwidth, or even meeting space and sandwiches should certainly be considered for membership. The technical aspects of catch and release are being solved, and it's up to everyone to work on the social details.

The NoCatAuth system is under active development. You can always get the latest version from *http://nocat.net*.

In Closing

802.11b hardware seems to be limited only by the imagination of those who can get their hands on it—and with prices dropping as time goes on, the number of people who are hacking it will only increase. If you're interested in extending the gear, sign on to any of the great local wireless mailing lists, buy yourself some gear, and get started.

## CHAPTER 8

Radio Free Planet

This past year has shown an explosion of interest in building wireless public networks. The ubiquity of affordable 802.11b gear has fueled enormous interest in extending the Net and providing open (or very low cost) access to it. The idea seems almost inevitable: if major wireless providers charge thirty dollars or more *per month* for low-speed, unreliable wireless network access, and tools are available to provide high-speed access yourself for very little cost, why not join in and make it happen? People all over the planet who have shared some part of the "unlimited free bandwidth everywhere" dream are building their own ubiquitous high-speed networks. By cooperating and using open standards, people are now building the infrastructure necessary to provide network access to thousands of simultaneous users, at very little cost to themselves. People everywhere are beginning to realize that this can be done more practically as a cooperative community service, rather than as a commercial venture with an ultimate cash profit motive.

When I started work on this book in early 2001, there were perhaps 10 well-known wireless groups in existence. As I write this, the wireless communities list at Personal Telco (*http://www.personaltelco.net/index.cgi/ WirelessCommunities*) lists more than 50 independent community wireless groups. Here are a few of the biggest and most unique projects that I've come across. While by no means comprehensive, this introduction should give you an idea of what's going on (maybe even in your own neighborhood).

Seattle Wireless

Seattle Wireless (*http://www.seattlewireless.net*) has taken on one of the most ambitious projects of any community group: they intend to build a fully routed Metropolitan Area Network, independent of any commercial service provider. To this end, they are setting up their own top-level DNS domains, allocating private IP addresses, setting up backbone nodes, and managing the roll-out of the network so that any wireless node will be able to reach any other, without ever needing to pass packets over a commercial network. As any backbone node is able to provide Internet gateway services, wireless clients can also access the Internet regardless of where they may physically be located in the city.

As the entire wireless network doesn't ever rely on the wire, it keeps the operating cost of the network fixed, and also could provide valuable communication services in the event of a major disaster (Seattle isn't exactly known for its stability, in many ways). Seattle has some unique geographical advantages that may help this approach: relatively few trees, many tall buildings, rolling hills, and a high concentration of technically capable alpha geeks. I'm sure the coffee doesn't hurt, either.

Their web site provides a terrific wealth of information, from network routing theory to antenna design. The Seattle Wireless web site was launched in September 2000. Since then, they have been mentioned or featured in over 35 publications, ranging from *Wired* magazine to *Le Monde*, a major newspaper in France. They also have a huge mailing list following and hold regular meetings. They are making things happen in the Great Northwest.

BAWUG

The Bay Area Wireless User's Group (*http://www.bawug.org*) is one of several wireless groups in the San Francisco Bay area. It grew out of PlayaNet, the free 802.11b network of Burning Man (see *http://www.playanet.org* and *http://www.burningman.com* for details). Since a huge percentage of Burning Man attendees are from San Francisco, it was only natural that the 10-day-a-year playa network geeks would want something to work on for the other 355.

While they focus primarily on education, the BAWUG group has made great contributions to the global wireless community through their web site and regular meetings. Members have facilitated group equipment buys, done some stellar work on solving the labyrinthine FCC Part 15, and are doing quite well to fulfill their collective mission:

> BAWUG provides help with developing infrastructure such as: mailing lists, labor, education, etc. including monthly meetings. Our current goal is to publish documents to assist the wireless community, secondary is to build a community grassroots network.

They have also just brought the first ever real-world Wireless Hardware comparison database online. This is a free (and invaluable) tool for anyone using commercial APs. They are collecting actual performance statistics and data (including range, throughput, cost, and ease of use) from every piece of hardware they can get their hands on. They are keeping the database current through user submissions. Be sure to check out their site for details. If you're ever in the SF Bay area, I highly recommend attending a meeting. They consistently draw 50+ people, and they have been host to an interesting collection of speakers, ranging from wireless industry jockeys to Internet startups to hardcore RF hacks. It has been well worth the two-hour drive from Sebastopol each time our group has attended.

Personal Telco

One of a couple of groups in the Portland, Oregon area, the Personal Telco Project (*http://www.personaltelco.net*) is also helping to build community in the Pacific Northwest. Like many of us, the founders are frustrated with exorbitant network access fees and horrifically unresponsive commercial support people. They are specifying a detailed hardware solution for all of their members, making node operation as simple as possible, and building out their network very rapidly.

They host a mailing list and a regular IRC channel (*#personaltelco* at *irc. openprojects.net*), and they were host to the first ever global Wireless Summit meeting (see Chapter 9 for some discussion of the Summit and *http:// www.personaltelco.net/index.cgi/SummitJune2001* for the online report). Their mailing list has been a great source of information and debate.

NYC Wireless

There is a tremendous effort in New York City to bring free Internet access nodes online. To quote their web site:

> The network is free as in 'free speech' and 'free beer'. Each access point is run independently by volunteers with their own equipment.

The NYC Wireless group has produced some outstanding content, including a Power over Ethernet HOWTO. They are also looking into the possibility of incorporating as a non-profit organization and offering resource distribution services to their members and other community groups. Their efforts haven't gone unnoticed in the popular press; they have even been featured on CNN for their work on setting up public network access.

They can be found online at *http://www.nycwireless.net*, where they host a FAQ, mailing list, node map, and other resources.

GBPPR

The Green Bay Professional Packet Radio group (from Green Bay, Wisconsin) is a rare group, coming at wireless networking from a solid background in radio technology. While they are not particularly focused on 802.11b, they have a huge wealth of information about radio design. Exotic technologies such as laser beam point-to-point links, fractal antenna designs, and home-brew spectrum analyzers are just some of the fun things you'll find at GBPPR. Their main page is online at *http://www.qsl.net/n9zia/index.html*.

They also host a bunch of insanely useful interactive calculation tools. If you need to figure out fresnel zone clearance, antenna tilt and bearing, or the amount of gain required to bridge a given distance, you must check out their free interactive radio design software. You can find them online at: *http:// www.gbonline.com/~multiplx/wireless/page09.html*. In particular, I have found their Wireless Network Link Analysis tool invaluable for estimating path loss and link budget (see Chapter 7 for some examples of how to calculate this for yourself, then use their great online tool to play "what if").

GAWD

The Shmoo Group is building GAWD, the Global Access Wireless Database. While not an actual wireless community group, the service they provide is very interesting. Their tool lets wireless providers and groups list the physical location and capabilities of their access points. The data is then searchable by provider, location, or even latitude/longitude. As I write this, they have 211 APs listed online. You can check out GAWD (and list your own node) at *http://www.shmoo.com/gawd/*.

Guerrilla.net

Not content to be bound to a particular wireless technology or even to provide Internet access, the Guerrilla.net group from Boston aims to keep the flow of information alive:

> As pressure is asserted upon the Internet from insecure individuals in the US Government, an *alternative* network is needed to insure that the free flow of information is not obstructed, captured, analyzed, modified, or logged. This is the main purpose of guerrilla.net... The free flow of private information is a REQUIREMENT of a free society.

They host an impressive technical library, including information about building antennas, setting up point-to-point and public access links, and wireless technologies from UHF through 10GHz. They list several radio modes and even plans for a 6dbi omni antenna. They can be found online at *http://www.guerrilla.net*.

Universal Wireless

The public access community network phenomenon is certainly not limited to North America. Nearly half of the wireless projects listed on the Personal Telco community list are based outside the United States. Projects have been started in England, Germany, Sweden, France, Finland, Holland, Australia, and many other countries. I have personally been contacted by people interested in un-wiring cities in Tibet, Canada, and Mexico. From every indication, the community wireless network seems to be an idea whose time has finally come.

CHAPTER 9

Radio Free Sebastopol

My first brush with 802.11b networking in the summer of 2000 demonstrated something very clear to me, even then: it was obvious that wireless connectivity was going to be a tremendously important technology. In the next year, dozens of local community wireless groups (and even a few commercial ventures) have sprung up, building usable networks over the air using 802.11b equipment. This is the story of how an idea to make our corporate network more flexible has evolved, and has become part of a worldwide movement to provide ubiquitous wireless network access.

OSCON 2000

My initial introduction to wireless networking was in Monterey, California, at OSCON (Open Source Conference) 2000. O'Reilly arranged free public wireless access for conference attendees. The tremendous flexibility of being able to connect to the network from anywhere led to all sorts of interesting, unforeseen interactions. For example, people attending a large talk could converse in real time over IRC and discuss the talk (and even critique the speaker) without raising their voices. They could use the Net as a resource when asking the speaker questions, to draw out very interesting points by way of real-time examples. With an instant messaging client, ubiquitous wireless made an effective, free, two-way paging system. (Rather than trying to use the overloaded PCS phone system, it was now possible to send a quick "Where do you want to meet for lunch?" message and get a response back instantly.) Conference attendees no longer had to return to their hotel rooms for dialup access, or be banished to a terminal room away from where the action was, just to check their email or refer to a web page. That was assuming, of course, that one had an 802.11b card and laptop handy. Personally, I had to wrestle a card away from a buddy who happened to have a spare. I realized that networking on borrowed time wouldn't cut it; I simply had to pack my own.

On returning from OSCON, there was much interest at O'Reilly in getting wireless networking going at the office. If that much flexibility could be put in place for very low cost, why weren't we using it in-house? If conference-goers could use the stuff to grill speakers for information more effectively, what could it do for our company meetings and presentations? And so, without even knowing my Direct Sequence from my Spread Spectrum, I started down the long, winding path of wireless networking.

The Campus

After setting up a couple of access points to cover our campus, and a crash course in WEP, MAC filtering, and closed networks, our fledgling 802.11b network was up. With relatively little effort and expense (about $3000 and a few hours work in all), we now had seamless coverage in all three of our buildings, complete with roaming between APs. The main O'Reilly offices in Sebastopol consist of three two-story buildings, covering an area about 450 by 150 feet. Using one Lucent AP-1000 in each building, and a small 5db omni at each AP, I was able to cover nearly all of the offices and conference rooms.

Early on in the process, one of our users noticed that they couldn't get online, even though they had a very strong signal. Upon checking their net-work settings, I realized that they hadn't set their ESSID, and so were associ-ating with any available network. It just so happened that the network with the strongest signal was coming from the business next door! I fired up Lucent's Site Map tool, and, sure enough, there was an existing 802.11b net-work immediately next door. After a quick conversation with their sysad-min, we decided on a channel numbering scheme that would minimize interference between the two networks. (This is exactly why a preliminary site survey is so important: even though you may not see antennas, a net-work may already exist in your area! Don't just assume that since wireless is new to you, it's new to your part of town.)

Now that our offices were saturated with access, with 50+ users up and hap-pily untethered, what could we do with it next? Naturally, more than a few eyes turned to the hotel and coffee shop across the street. If one could get a signal from the hotel, then visiting employees who stayed there could get online for free, at 11Mbps (as opposed to paying for a trickle of dialup access). And of course, being able to work directly from the coffee shop must do *something* for productivity. With visions of mochas and bandwidth danc-ing in my head, I looked into adding external antennas to increase our range.

Coffee, Coffee, Coffee

In about a week, I had an omnidirectional antenna installed on the roof, running down 25 feet of LMR-200 to our access point. Why did I use 25 feet of cable that loses almost 17db of signal every hundred feet? And why did I use an omni, when a tight sector or patch antenna would have made more sense? Because a year ago, without any prior background in radio, I went with what our vendor had to offer: a 25-foot run of so-called "low-loss" microwave antenna cable and an expensive omnidirectional popsicle stick. (After all, if Lucent made the gear, it *must* be compatible with a Lucent access point, right?)

Luckily for me, even with the high line loss, the omni managed to do the job. That afternoon, I walked across the street, ordered an iced mocha, and merrily typed out the confirmation email. As I hit *Control-X Y*, I was compelled to meditate on that inevitable question, "What next?" If it was possible to get a good signal about 1500 feet from the AP, how feasible would it be to provide wireless access to our local employees? After all, many of our people live in the area and were using dialup to access our network from home. Would it be possible to provide a fast wireless connection to anyone who was within range? Just how far could this technology be stretched?

Online from Home, No Strings Attached

Around this time, I relocated to Sebastopol from San Francisco. By a staggering coincidence, the house we moved into happened to have a clean line of sight to the antenna I installed on the roof, more than half a mile away. This provided a great tool for experimentation, as I now had a fixed signal at a distance with clear LOS and could aim whatever kind of equipment I liked at it to see how well it would perform. I realized that a high-gain dish, pointed directly at the omni, could achieve a very good signal, even through walls and glass. I was so excited by the quality of the signal that I bungee-corded the dish to a chair with rollers, and rolled it around the house, while streaming a full-screen video on my laptop the entire time. Yes, a keen interest in wireless was now developing into a full-blown psychotic obsession, as the potential possibilities of long-distance, low-cost, high-speed communications played about in my mind.

I finally mounted the dish inside my attic, set up a makeshift access point, and found that I could have a stable 11Mbps connection from about six-tenths of a mile away, with a "stealth" dish under my roof that wouldn't bother the neighbors. I used this connection for several months, through all kinds of weather (and I was very grateful of it: in my area, DSL and cable modems weren't an option at the time).

Now that I had a proof-of-concept and parts list, I approached others in the company who live in the area, to try to set up a second node. This was when I came up against possibly the biggest natural obstacle to long distance microwave: *trees*. As it turned out, I had been truly lucky with my own situation. Finding many clean paths to a single point is highly improbable in Sebastopol. Except for the immediate downtown area, medium to dense foliage is virtually everywhere. After visiting several possible node sites (and trying to shoot to O'Reilly despite the trees), it became clear that a single access point at a low altitude wasn't going to be sufficient to get our Sebastopol employees unplugged. There are just too many trees between O'Reilly and the rest of the world.

With no obvious plan of action, I had to put the wireless extension project away for a while so I could do more research. By now, there was certainly no shortage of online information available, as community groups began popping up all over the globe. I decided that if I was going to get anywhere with practical wireless networking, I'd need to talk to some experts.

Seattle Wireless

Last March, I took a trip to Seattle. My brother was moving to the area, and so I took the opportunity to travel with him up north to see the Seattle Wireless network for myself. I must admit that wasn't fully prepared (psychologically) for what I found when I got there. Here were a bunch of *very* sharp sysadmins, programmers, and net monkeys, who were gearing up to build a redundant, fully routed public network, independent of the Internet. They were working on this project *entirely in their spare time*, with no promise of reward other than the joy of hacking out a project that simply needed to be done. They weren't just hooking up a couple of APs and trusting their luck; they had an entire network topology planned, a hardware solution down, and nodes in the works to connect sites miles apart.

I spent a day building antennas and speculating about the possibilities of 802.11b with the SWN crowd. By the end of the day, we managed to put together a yagi made out of washers, some tubing, a bolt, and a pie tin that carried an 11Mbps signal about a mile. The topology of Seattle is such that their network plans will probably work: tall buildings, rolling hills, and limited tree cover make much of the city accessible (assuming one can get on top of the hills). I went back to Sebastopol with a few important realizations:

- There was tremendous interest in high-speed wireless networking, even among people who already had high-speed wired access. Ubiquitous wireless seemed to be almost as much in demand as DSL and cable modems.

- The seemingly insurmountable difficulty of finding LOS between points can't really be approached by one person or group. But a larger community, working together toward the same goal, can bring a lot of resources to bear on any problem.

- Wireless networking isn't as simple as replacing a piece of CAT5 with a radio. Radio has many strange properties that are completely alien to people who have been studying computers and networking for years.

- Conversely, many radio experts find themselves lost when dealing with the intricacies of Internet networking (until very recently, a 9600-baud packet radio connection to a computer running a DOS TCP/IP stack was considered high tech in many circles). If we intend to push 802.11b beyond its intended limits, the plateau of knowledge that separates hardcore network jockeys from hardcore radio geeks *must* be crossed.

Ironically, it started to look like it would be easier to get the entire Sebastopol area unplugged with open network access, rather than trying to connect a few users to a private network. But to do that, I certainly couldn't do all of the work. I needed to find out if there was as much interest in my area as there seemed to be in the rest of the country.

NoCat

It was obvious that we needed a local repository for information about forming a cooperative community network. Within a couple of days, some friends and I put together a simple web site and mailing list. But what to call it?

While sitting on the couch in the living room, logging in to check on something at work, my login fortune struck me as particularly funny, so I read it aloud to my friend Cat:

> You see, wire telegraph is a kind of a very, very long cat. You pull his tail in New York and his head is meowing in Los Angeles. Do you understand this? And radio operates exactly the same way: you send signals here, they receive them there. The only difference is that there is *no cat*. –Albert Einstein

Cat quickly replied, "That's what you should call this thing: No Cat." I immediately checked *whois* and saw that *nocat.net* was free. That settled it.

NoCat became the central repository for several wireless projects that Schuyler Erle (Perl programmer extraordinaire and wireless sympathizer from O'Reilly), myself, and others had been working on. We put together WRP, a wireless router-on-a-floppy to make setting up a wireless gateway quick and painless. We also started work on the NoCatAuth project, a method for authenticating users to a cooperative network without using any of the built-in (and limited) authentication methods available in the 802.11b spec. We also set up a mailing list for locals interested in wireless. Now that we had a web presence and some information available, we needed a way to connect with people in the local community.

The Article

Luckily, we didn't have to wait very long for the community to notice us. Just after I returned from Seattle, a local newspaper (the *Press Democrat*, see *http://www.pressdemo.com/business/columns/02sims.html*) ran a feature on some of the wireless shenanigans I had been up to. I had no idea at the time how valuable this kind of exposure could be to the community LAN idea. Within a week, I had received a few dozen emails and several phone calls from locals who were interested in wireless networking. Some offered expertise and equipment, while others were simply curious about our plans and what could be accomplished with 802.11b.

After the article ran, our mailing list grew to about 25 people. We decided to hold a general meeting to get organized and figure out what we wanted to do with this stuff. I was very pleasantly surprised when 16 interested people showed up at that first meeting. Many were looking for free high-speed access, while others were simply curious. A few were Northpoint victims who had been forcibly unplugged from their DSL when that company went under and who were looking for any alternative (apparently, they were no longer considered part of the "prime" market and would likely not see high-speed access again for quite a while).

As the discussion went well into the third hour, it was obvious from that first meeting that this was going to turn into a regular event. These people were keenly interested in contributing to a free local network, and they had a tremendous amount of knowledge and resources among them. But until now, they had no good way of connecting with each other. From this first get-together, all sorts of possibilities began to present themselves.

The general consensus was that, if people who had high-speed Net access wanted to share with those who wanted it but, for whatever reason, could not get it, there were several technical obstacles that needed to be overcome:

- The solution couldn't cost thousands of dollars, or else no one could afford it.
- There had to be a secure and easy way of figuring out who was who and limiting what users could do on the network (so that node owners wouldn't be exposed to abusers or have their hard-earned bandwidth monopolized by a freeloading few).
- The solution needed to be simple enough for someone with limited skills to set up, and it needed to require little or no maintenance.

- There had to be an easy way for people interested in point-to-point links to meet with each other.

- People who did have a fair idea of how to proceed needed access to all sorts of information, from choosing microwave connectors to configuring laptops.

We had some answers to these issues, but it became clear that these were going to be long-term problems, shared by anyone attempting to put together a community group. We put as much information as we could up at NoCat and pointed to others who had answers whenever possible.

The nearest wireless community group to Sebastopol was the BAWUG, who met regularly in the San Jose area. Since we were obviously working along parallel lines, it seemed to be time to see what our neighbors to the south were up to. I got a couple of local wireless zealots together, and together we made the two-hour trek to San Jose for a meeting.

The June 2001 BAWUG meeting was a great opportunity to network further. Much like our Sebastopol meeting, there were people with all different abilities and expectations present (only here there were about fifty of them!). After a couple of interesting presentations, I got a chance to talk with antenna gurus, some Apple AirPort hackers, and even a commercial wireless startup.

There was much buzz about the impending Portland Summit meeting. Wireless community leaders from all over were going to converge on Portland for a weekend of planning, talk, beer, and general hackery. This was a meeting I could not miss.

The Portland Summit

Last June, for the first time ever, people from community wireless networks across the country (and even from Canada!) met in Portland to talk about what we were up to. Organizers from Seattle, New York, British Columbia, Portland, the San Francisco Bay area, and Sebastopol were there. We had a very productive couple of days, covering divergent topics such as antenna design, network layout, the FCC, and "catch and release" captive portals. There was a tremendous energy and goodwill between the groups, as we all realized we were in this experiment together (admittedly, the beer probably helped a bit, too).

I think the Portland Summit was very reassuring for all of us. Here we had people from all over the globe who share something of a common vision: unlimited free bandwidth everywhere. We developed these ideas independently, and while some of the details of how we were attempting this feat diverged, the ultimate intent was the same. Wireless community network access seems to be an idea whose time has finally come; hardware, software, and network backbone are all becoming cheap and ubiquitous enough to make it happen. All of our groups want to strengthen our local communities by bringing network access to anyone who cares to be a part of it. And by working together, sharing what we've learned, giving away software, and pooling our collective efforts, we are finding that we can reach this goal faster than by trying to work out a solution on our own.

The Future

Now, with about 150 people on the mailing list, regular monthly meetings, and an ever increasing number of public access nodes, we are definitely moving toward ubiquitous, free network access for whoever wants to use it. The NoCatAuth software has been officially released (check out *http://nocat. net* for details), and the priority in Sebastopol is now to get nodes online.

With cooperative effort and wireless technology, the Internet is rapidly becoming more and more pervasive. My direct experience with people working on this project has turned up an important common thread: free access to information is in constant demand, and barriers to that access cause pain. I believe that working to provide free, unrestricted access to the Internet is a benefit not only to one's local community, but also to the world at large. I hope that this book has helped you to realize your goals and has helped you become more connected to your local community.

Appendix

Path Loss Calculations

Here's a simple table of path loss calculations in free space for channels 1 and 11, with clear line of sight. See Chapter 6 for how to use these numbers to figure out how far your network can reach. Distances are in miles, losses are in dB.

Distance (miles)	2.412 GHz (ch. 1)	2.462 GHz (ch. 11)
0.5	98.2	98.4
1	104.2	104.4
2	110.3	110.4
3	113.8	114.0
4	116.3	116.5
5	118.2	118.4
7	121.1	121.3
10	124.2	124.4
15	127.8	127.9
20	130.3	130.4
25	132.2	132.4
30	133.8	134.0

This path loss table was calculated with the following formula, rounded up to the nearest tenth:

$$L = 20 \log(d) + 20 \log(f) + 36.6$$

For possibly the most authoritative source of radio information on the planet, check out the ARRL online at *http://www.arrl.org*, or see any of their excellent books (in particular, their *UHF/Microwave Experimenter's Manual* and *Antenna Book* are definitive sources for learning about microwave communications).

Links to Community Wireless Sites

The community wireless phenomenon is happening all over the globe. There is a good list of projects up at *http://www.toaster.net/wireless/community. html*. A few of the major networks (and our humble Sebastopol co-op) are listed below. If there isn't a community group in your area, start one yourself! I was certainly surprised at the broad range of people interested in setting up communications. Get the word out, start a mailing list, and get connected to your community. The resources that a community can pull together for a common project are astounding. You simply have to do it!

Seattle Wireless (Seattle, WA)
   http://seattlewireless.net

Bay Area Wireless Users Group (San Francisco Bay, CA)
   http://www.bawug.org

Personal Telco Project (Portland, OR)
   http://www.personaltelco.net

NYC Wireless (New York, NY)
   http://www.nycwireless.net

GBPPR (Green Bay, WI)
   http://www.qsl.net/n9zia/index.htm

Guerrilla.Net (Cambridge, MA)
   http://www.guerrilla.net

NoCat (Sebastopol, CA)
   http://nocat.net

FCC Part 15 Rules

Radio emissions in the U.S. are refereed by the FCC. In Title 47, Chapter I, Part 15, Subpart C, Section 15.247, rules pertaining to unlicensed operations in the 2.4GHz range are outlined.

The full text of Part 15 (and most other sections of US federal code) can be browsed online at *http://www.access.gpo.gov/nara/cfr/cfr-table-search.html*.

For a good discussion (and interesting interpretation) of the rules and how they pertain specifically to 802.11b, take a look at Tim Pozar's excellent report for the BAWUG, available online at *http://www.lns.com/papers/ FCCPart15_and_the_ISM_2.4G_Band.index*.

From the U.S. Government Printing Office via GPO Access
[CITE: 47CFR15.247]

TITLE 47--TELECOMMUNICATION
CHAPTER I--FEDERAL COMMUNICATIONS COMMISSION
PART 15--RADIO FREQUENCY DEVICES--Table of Contents
Subpart C--Intentional Radiators
Sec. 15.247 Operation within the bands 902-928 MHz, 2400-2483.5 MHz, and 5725-5850 MHz.

(a) Operation under the provisions of this section is limited to frequency hopping and direct sequence spread spectrum intentional radiators that comply with the following provisions:

(1) Frequency hopping systems shall have hopping channel carrier frequencies separated by a minimum of 25 kHz or the 20 dB bandwidth of the hopping channel, whichever is greater. The system shall hop to channel frequencies that are selected at the system hopping rate from a pseudorandomly ordered list of hopping frequencies. Each frequency must be used equally on the average by each transmitter. The system receivers shall have input bandwidths that match the hopping channel bandwidths of their corresponding transmitters and shall shift frequencies in synchronization with the transmitted signals.

(i) For frequency hopping systems operating in the 902-928 MHz band: if the 20 dB bandwidth of the hopping channel is less than 250 kHz, the system shall use at least 50 hopping frequencies and the average time of occupancy on any frequency shall not be greater than 0.4 seconds within a 20 second period; if the 20 dB bandwidth of the hopping channel is 250 kHz or greater, the system shall use at least 25 hopping frequencies and the average time of occupancy on any frequency shall not be greater than 0.4 seconds within a 10 second period. The maximum allowed 20 dB bandwidth of the hopping channel is 500 kHz.

(ii) Frequency hopping systems operating in the 2400-2483.5 MHz and 5725-5850 MHz bands shall use at least 75 hopping frequencies. The maximum 20 dB bandwidth of the hopping channel is 1 MHz. The average time of occupancy on any frequency shall not be greater than 0.4 seconds within a 30 second period.

(iii) Frequency hopping systems in the 2400-2483.5 MHz band may utilize hopping channels whose 20 dB bandwidth is greater than 1 MHz provided the systems use at least 15 non-overlapping channels. The total span of hopping channels shall be at least 75 MHz. The average time of occupancy on any one channel shall not be greater than 0.4 seconds within the time period required to hop through all channels.

(2) For direct sequence systems, the minimum 6 dB bandwidth shall be at least 500 kHz.

(b) The maximum peak output power of the intentional radiator shall not exceed the following:

(1) For frequency hopping systems in the 2400-2483.5 MHz band employing at least 75 hopping channels, all frequency hopping systems in the 5725-5850 MHz band, and all direct sequence systems: 1 watt. For all other frequency hopping systems in the 2400-2483.5 MHz band: 0.125 watts.

(2) For frequency hopping systems operating in the 902-928 MHz band: 1 watt for systems employing at least 50 hopping channels; and, 0.25 watts for systems employing less than 50 hopping channels, but at least 25 hopping channels, as permitted under paragraph (a)(1)(i) of this section.

(3) Except as shown in paragraphs (b)(3) (i), (ii) and (iii) of this section, if transmitting antennas of directional gain greater than 6 dBi are used the peak output power from the intentional radiator shall be reduced below the stated values in paragraphs (b)(1) or (b)(2) of this section, as appropriate, by the amount in dB that the directional gain of the antenna exceeds 6 dBi.

(i) Systems operating in the 2400-2483.5 MHz band that are used exclusively for fixed, point-to-point operations may employ transmitting antennas with directional gain greater than 6 dBi provided the maximum peak output power of the intentional radiator is reduced by 1 dB for every 3 dB that the directional gain of the antenna exceeds 6 dBi.

(ii) Systems operating in the 5725-5850 MHz band that are used exclusively for fixed, point-to-point operations may employ transmitting antennas with directional gain greater than 6 dBi without any corresponding reduction in transmitter peak output power.

(iii) Fixed, point-to-point operation, as used in paragraphs (b)(3)(i) and (b)(3)(ii) of this section, excludes the use of point-to-multipoint systems, omnidirectional applications, and multiple co-located intentional radiators transmitting the same information. The operator of the spread spectrum intentional radiator or, if the equipment is professionally installed, the installer is responsible for ensuring that the system is used exclusively for fixed, point-to-point operations. The instruction manual furnished with the intentional radiator shall contain language in the installation instructions informing the operator and the installer of this responsibility.

(4) Systems operating under the provisions of this section shall be operated in a manner that ensures that the public is not exposed to radio frequency energy levels in excess of the Commission's guidelines. See Sec. 1.1307(b)(1) of this chapter.

(c) In any 100 kHz bandwidth outside the frequency band in which the spread spectrum intentional radiator is operating, the radio frequency power that is produced by the intentional radiator shall be at least 20 dB below that in the 100 kHz bandwidth within the band that contains the highest level of the desired power, based on either an RF conducted or a radiated measurement. Attenuation below the general limits specified in Sec. 15.209(a) is not required. In addition, radiated emissions which fall in the restricted bands, as defined in Sec. 15.205(a), must also comply with the radiated emission limits specified in Sec. 15.209(a) (see Sec. 15.205(c)).

(d) For direct sequence systems, the peak power spectral density conducted from the intentional radiator to the antenna shall not be greater than 8 dBm in any 3 kHz band during any time interval of continuous transmission.

(e) The processing gain of a direct sequence system shall be at least 10 dB. The processing gain represents the improvement to the received signal-to-noise ratio, after filtering to the information bandwidth, from the spreading/despreading function. The processing gain may be determined using one of the following methods:

(1) As measured at the demodulated output of the receiver: the ratio in dB of the signal-to-noise ratio with the system spreading code turned off to the signal-to-noise ratio with the system spreading code turned on.

(2) As measured using the CW jamming margin method: a signal generator is stepped in 50 kHz increments across the passband of the system, recording at each point the generator level required to produce the recommended Bit Error Rate (BER). This level is the jammer level. The output power of the intentional radiator is measured at the same point. The jammer to signal ratio (J/S) is then calculated, discarding the worst 20% of the J/S data points. The lowest remaining J/S ratio is used to calculate the processing gain, as follows: $Gp = (S/N)o + Mj + Lsys$, where Gp = processing gain of the system, $(S/N)o$ = signal to noise ratio required for the chosen BER, Mj = J/S ratio, and Lsys = system losses. Note that total losses in a system, including intentional radiator and receiver, should be assumed to be no more than 2 dB.

(f) Hybrid systems that employ a combination of both direct sequence and frequency hopping modulation techniques shall achieve a processing gain of at least 17 dB from the combined techniques. The frequency hopping operation of the hybrid system, with the direct sequence operation turned off, shall have an average time of occupancy on any frequency not to exceed 0.4 seconds within a time period in seconds equal to the number of hopping frequencies employed multiplied by 0.4. The direct sequence operation of the hybrid system, with the frequency hopping operation turned off, shall comply with the power density requirements of paragraph (d) of this section.

(g) Frequency hopping spread spectrum systems are not required to employ all available hopping channels during each transmission. However, the system, consisting of both the transmitter and the receiver, must be designed to comply with all of the regulations in this section should the transmitter be presented with a continuous data (or information) stream. In addition, a system employing short transmission bursts must comply with the definition of a frequency hopping system and must distribute its transmissions over the minimum number of hopping channels specified in this section.

(h) The incorporation of intelligence within a frequency hopping spread spectrum system that permits the system to recognize other users within the spectrum band so that it individually and independently chooses and adapts its hopsets to avoid hopping on occupied channels is permitted. The coordination of frequency hopping systems in any other manner for the express purpose of avoiding the simultaneous occupancy of individual hopping frequencies by multiple transmitters is not permitted.

Note: Spread spectrum systems are sharing these bands on a noninterference basis with systems supporting critical Government requirements that have been allocated the usage of these bands, secondary only to ISM equipment operated under the provisions of part 18 of this chapter. Many of these Government systems are airborne radiolocation systems that emit a high

EIRP which can cause interference to other users. Also, investigations of the effect of spread spectrum interference to U. S. Government operations in the 902-928 MHz band may require a future decrease in the power limits allowed for spread spectrum operation.

[54 FR 17714, Apr. 25, 1989, as amended at 55 FR 28762, July 13, 1990; 62 FR 26242, May 13, 1997; 65 FR 57561, Sept. 25, 2000]

Simple Scheme Management

Here's a simple method for managing your network schemes on Linux. You will need *sudo* installed and will need *sudo* privileges to run */sbin/cardctl*.

Create the following shell script called *scheme*:

```
#!/bin/sh

SCHEME=`/usr/bin/basename $0`

if [ "$SCHEME" == "scheme" ]; then
  unset SCHEME
fi

/usr/bin/sudo /sbin/cardctl scheme $SCHEME
```

Install the script somewhere in your PATH (I put mine in *~/bin*). Then make symlinks to the script with the names of schemes you want to access quickly, in the same directory:

```
rob@entropy:~/bin$ ln -s scheme home
rob@entropy:~/bin$ ln -s scheme oreilly
rob@entropy:~/bin$ ln -s scheme nocat
rob@entropy:~/bin$ ln -s scheme any
```

Now, make matching entries in your */etc/pcmcia/wireless.opts:*

```
home,*,*,*)
    INFO="IBSS net at Home"
    ESSID="HomeNet"
    MODE="Ad-Hoc"
    KEY="1234-5678-90"
    RATE="11M"
    ;;

oreilly,*,*,*)
    INFO="Work"
    ESSID="OReillyNet"
    MODE="Managed"
    KEY="s:sHHHH"
    IWCONFIG="power unicast"
    ;;

nocat,*,*,*)
    INFO="NoCat Community net"
```

```
    ESSID="NoCat"
    MODE="Managed"
    ;;

any,*,*,*)
    INFO="Default configuration"
    ESSID="ANY"
    MODE="Managed"
    ;;
```

Now, when you want to change schemes quickly, just type *home* or *any* to instantly change all of your wireless and network settings. As an added bonus, typing *scheme* will show the current scheme. Keep in mind that *sudo* will prompt you for your password, as you will need to be root to change the scheme.

Index

We'd like to hear your suggestions for improving our indexes. Send email to *index@oreilly.com*.

B

Basic Service Set (BSS) mode, 16
BAWUG (Bay Area Wireless User's Group), 100, 110
Bay Area Wireless User's Group (see BAWUG)
Bayonet Navy Connector (BNC), 71
Belden, 70
Bluetooth equipment, 3
BNC (Bayonet Navy Connector), 71
Bridging Functions tab (AirPort), 38
bridging wireless networks, 91
BSS (Basic Service Set) mode, 16
burglar alarms, 3
Burning Man, 100

C

cables, 70
    range, calculating for, 76–79
captive portals, implementing, 94
cardctl scheme command (PCMCIA), 49
cardctl status command (PCMCIA), 50
cards (wireless), 90–91
catch and release (captive portal), 94–98
caveats (access point), 32–34
cell phones, setting up point-to-point links with, 82
channel frequencies for 802.11b, 12
channel spacings, 41
Cisco Aironet 350, 32
Clapp, Andrew, 83
client radios, 13
cliproxy (RG configuration utility), 35, 39
Closed network box (AirPort), 40
closed networks, 18, 39
Community name field (AirPort), 35
Configurator (AirPort), 35
connections, establishing, 93
connectors, 71–75
    range, calculating for, 76–79
Co-op Classes, 96
cooperatives for WISP, 5
cordless phones, 3
Cygwin package, 93

D

default password for Airport, 35
DeLorme's TopoUSA 2.0, 59
Device address field (AirPort), 35
DHCP (Dynamic Host Configuration Protocol), 16, 20–21, 96
    access points and, 31
    AirPort and, 37
    Functions tab (AirPort), 37
    peer-to-peer services, 54
dhcpd packages, 55
dialup, configuring for AirPort, 36
Digital Orthophoto Quadrangles (DOQs), 14
Digital Subscriber Line (DSL), 1
Direct Sequence Spread Spectrum (see DSSS)
Discover Devices button (AirPort), 35
dishes (Parabolic), 67
Distribute addresses on Ethernet port (AirPort), 37
distributions of prebuilt Linux networks, 57
D-Link DWL-1000AP, 32
DNS (Domain Name Server), 16, 21
Domain Name Server (see DNS)
DOQs (Digital Orthophoto Quadrangles), 14
DSL (Digital Subscriber Line), 1
DSSS (Direct Sequence Spread Spectrum), 2
Dynamic Host Configuration Protocol (see DHCP)

E

electrical waves, 88
email, securing, 93
encryption, 40
    end-to-end, 93
    tunnels, 27
    WEP (see WEP)
end-to-end encryption, 93
Erle, Schuyler, 108
ESS (Extended Service Set), 17
ESSID (Extended Service ID), 17
    access points and, 33
ethereal (protocol analysis tool), 33
Ethernet, 16
experience, 24

Extended Service ID (ESSID), 17
    access points and, 33
Extended Service Set (ESS), 17
external antennas, 18

F

FHSS (Frequency Hopping Spread
        Spectrum), 2
firewalls, 26
    tools, 45
frequencies for 802.11b, 12
Frequency Hopping Spread Spectrum
        (see FHSS)
Fujitsu Stylistic 1000 repeater, 90

G

gateways, 96
    building on Linux, 43–57
GAWD (Global Access Wireless
        Database), 102
GBPPR group (Green Bay Professional
        Packet Radio), 77, 102
geographical diversity, dealing
        with, 59–62
Global Access Wireless Database (see
        GAWD)
Gnome window manager, 45
GPS hardware
    point-to-point links and, 81
    using Topo map software, 59
Green Bay Professional Packet Radio
        group (see GBPPR)
Guerrilla.net group, 102

H

hardware
    requirements for projects, 9
    for wireless gateways on
        Linux, 43–45
Hardware HOWTO, 44
heliax microwave cabling, 70
HP/UX, 93

I

IANA (Internet Assigned Numbers
        Authority), 22
IBSS (Independent Basic Service Set)
        mode, 16

IEEE Standards Committee, 2
ifconfig PCMCIA tool, 51
Independent Basic Service Set mode (see
        IBSS)
infrastructure (wireless), 16–20
Intel 2011, 32
Internet Assigned Numbers Authority
        (see IANA)
Internet Software Consortium, 54
ISPs (Internet Service Providers), 3
iwconfig PCMCIA tool, 51
iwlist PCMCIA tool, 51
iwpriv PCMCIA tool, 51
iwspy PCMCIA tool, 51

J

Java Configurator for AirPort, 35
Java Runtime Environment, managing
        access point software, 35

K

KDE window manager, 45
kernel configuration, 46–48
keys (WEP), 33, 40

L

LAN access, 36
laptops, using as a gateway, 44
Le Monde magazine, 100
Line of Sight (see LOS)
link budgets, 76
links
    point-to-point, 80
    redundant, 88
Linksys WAP-11, 32, 81
Linux
    access point software, managing
        for, 35, 39
    distribution, 45
    installing, 45
    kernel configuration, 46–48
    OpenSSH and, 93
    PCMCIA slots, 90
    prebuild distributions, 57
    wireless gateways, building
        with, 43–57
LMR cable, 70
Local LAN access, 36

Press Democrat (newspaper), 109
Pringles cans, fitting antennas
            inside, 83–88
project scope, defining, 8–15
    hardware requirements, 9
    potential coverage problem areas, 13
Public Class users, 95

R

radio cards, 16
radio repeaters, 90
radios, setting up point-to-point links
            with, 82
ranges for antennas, calculating, 76–79
receiver sensitivity specs, 77
redundant links, 88
repeaters (radio), 90
residential gateway, 19
Retrieve Settings button (AirPort), 35
RG configuration utility (cliproxy), 35
roaming, 40
routing, 26

S

Samba, 45
Seattle Wireless, 99, 107
Sebastopol (California), 59, 104–111
sector antenna (sectoral), 67
security, 24, 92–94
    peer-to-peer networking and, 55
servers (DHCP), 54
Sevy, Jon, 35
Shmoo Group, 102
signals, 10
    loss in antenna adapters, 65
Silver cards in Apple AirPort, 34
Site Monitor tool (Lucent), 13
site survey of network project, 10
SMA/SMC connectors, 73
software, 13
    for access point management, 35
    geographical diversity, dealing
            with, 59–60
    PCMCIA devices, 48
Solaris, 93
spectrum analyzers, 13
SSH tunnels, 29
SSL connections, 28
    security concerns and, 93

T

tcpdump (protocol analysis tool), 33
TCP/IP services, 16
Times Microwave, 70
TNC connectors, 72, 81
tools (wireless), 51
Topo maps, 59–62
topographical mapping, 14
Tourrilhes, Jean, 51
transparent bridges, 38
tunnels (encryption), 27

U

UHF connectors, 73
USGS, 14

W

WEP (wired equivalent privacy)
            encryption, 17, 25, 82, 92
    AirPort, using, 39
    peer-to-peer networks, 55
wide area network saturation, 58–79
    geographical diversity, 59–62
Windows, 93
wired equivalent privacy (see WEP)
Wired magazine, 100
wireless cards, 90–91
wireless community networks, 1–7
    access points, using, 31–41
    layout of, 16–30
    peer-to-peer networking, 42–57
    project scope, defining, 8–15
    wide area network saturation, 58–79
Wireless LAN Settings tab (AirPort), 40
Wireless Network Link Analysis (Green
            Bay Professional Packet
            Radio), 77
wireless X-10 cameras, 3
WISPs (Wireless Internet Service
            Providers), 4
WRP wireless router-on-a-floppy, 108

X

X Windows, 45
X-10 cameras, 3

Y

yagi antennas, 67, 83